*Confronting Religious Oppression ... g
Re-Examination of Scripture and History*

RELEASING
THE CAPTIVE
Woman

Shanna i..
"Shamona"
or ~ my
May you have an
ABUNDANT life.
Dianne Emilia

Dianne Emilia St. Jean

RELEASING THE CAPTIVE WOMAN
Copyright © 2014 by Dianne Emilia St. Jean

Scripture quotations, unless otherwise marked, are taken from the New King James Version®. Copyright © 1982 by Thomas Nelson, Inc. Used by permission. All rights reserved. • Scripture quotations (marked CJB) are taken from the Complete Jewish Bible, copyright © 1998 by David H. Stern. Published by Jewish New Testament Publications, Inc. www.messianicjewish.net/jntp. Distributed by Messianic Jewish Resources. www.messianicjewish.net. All rights reserved. Used by permission.

Printed in Canada

ISBN: 978-1-77069-779-9

Word Alive Press
131 Cordite Road, Winnipeg, MB R3W 1S1
www.wordalivepress.ca

Library and Archives Canada Cataloguing in Publication

St. Jean, Dianne Emilia, 1958-
     Releasing the captive woman : confronting religious oppression through re-examination of scripture and history / Dianne Emilia St. Jean.

ISBN 978-1-77069-779-9

     1. Divorced women--Religious life. 2. Separated women--Religious life. 3. Remarried people--Religious life. 4. Spiritual life. I. Title.

BL625.7.E65 2014   200.82   C2012-907811-5

My eyes make me so upset at the fate of the women in my city.

Lamentations 3:51 (CJB)

INTRODUCTION

There is a prayer that goes up night and day from the hearts of millions of women. It is a plea for death—either her own, or that of her oppressor. It is the Prayer of the Chained Woman, she who lacks the means or strength to escape the life in which she is trapped and therefore sees no other way out except through death.

This statement may seem dramatic, but its intensity and truth is as real on the face of this earth as surely as the sun rises each day. Some of these women live within cultures that deny them access to personal or legal support. Others live within societies that do provide options, yet many women do not take advantage of them. Why? The reality is that even in societies where women have laws behind them many continue to be controlled, manipulated, or threatened against taking any action that will free them.

The struggle for freedom is not only on the outside of her world. Some of the strongest chains that keep women bound go far deeper, into the heart and mind. These are the chains of fear and wrong thinking. The minute she begins to seriously consider escaping from her situation, thoughts start rushing in: she will not be allowed to take her children, or she will not be able to support them. In even more difficult scenarios, her life or the life of her loved ones will be threatened with harm or death. There are also thoughts of emotional obligation or pity (what she perceives to be love) that make her feel guilty for disappointing or abandoning the very person who is mistreating her. Sometimes the woman's emotional insecurities tell her that she might as well stay because, after all, she should be grateful to at least have somebody. This stems from the feelings of personal unworthiness usually found in women who have been subjected to rejection or constant negative labeling.

There are many books which address issues of neglect and abuse in relationships; however, women in these situations who also embrace a deep faith or religious conviction face a unique dilemma. They often feel they are restricted to only two choices, both which put them in a lose/lose situation: either they tolerate the conditions of the relationship in order to remain in the faith (especially if they associate their faith community with the mindset of God), or they must set aside their convictions in order to leave the relationship. Women who, for whatever reason, cannot bring themselves to leave often reconcile the conflict of their decision by convincing themselves that remaining in the relationship is their personal sacrifice or duty. Somehow, someday, God will reward them for their suffering and their faithfulness.

Most books advocated by religious institutions tend to justify that position. If a marital situation is bad enough and a woman of faith does decide to leave, she often finds herself being judged by members of her faith community, and she becomes the subject of their gossip. Sometimes she is accused of being unforgiving toward her husband; some are even told that their problems will evaporate if they would just learn to be more submissive. In other words, the blame is put back on the victim. The most extreme judgment, however, is when the woman is told that if she does leave her husband, God will punish or abandon her because she is sinning.

Unfortunately, well-intended yet misguided advice is not restricted to faith advisors. Sometimes secular counselors encourage these women to abandon their personal beliefs along with the relationship, perceiving "religion" to be the core of the problem. Either way, both secular and religious counselors *place the burden of failure on the woman,* making *her* beliefs and actions the culprit rather than the offending spouse. In other words, one side says, "You don't have enough faith," while the other says, "Your problems are caused by your faith." Consequently, many women feel they must choose between their faith in God and their freedom—yet another wrangling added to their personal battles.

This brings us to the question: Can a woman of faith wanting to leave an abusive or oppressive marriage truly remain in that faith? Having experienced the chains of marital abuse and neglect, I have asked myself that question over the years and have desperately sought for answers. As an individual of deep conviction, I could not bring myself to renounce my faith in God, nor could I reconcile myself to believe that the heart of this God would command women who unexpectedly find themselves in that situation to remain locked in misery forever.

This book is written for such women. It explores the dynamics of being trapped in an oppressive relationship and struggling morally and mentally with the thought of leaving or having left, perhaps also suffering at the hands of others for doing so. It also addresses the mindset of those within faith communities who have the power to either free the oppressed person or keep them bound. Unfortunately it is not only men who contribute to this oppression but also women who see it as a religious duty. Either they have had a tolerable, if not fulfilling, marriage experience and therefore cannot identify with women who are suffering in that situation, or they themselves have experienced marital misery but are convinced that tolerating it was the right and only thing to do. Instead of helping their oppressed sister, they talk her down into mute submission.

This book is also written for those who claim they are not "religious" yet adhere to attitudes and beliefs that keep women bound and manipulated. These attitudes are not restricted to religious institutions but have permeated mainstream society to the point that they are often accepted as the norm. For this reason we will be exploring viewpoints toward women throughout history, including those before the development of mainstream religions such as Judaism, Christianity, and Islam.

Nonetheless, much of the justification behind the mistreatment of females in general, even in the modern world, stems from interpretations of certain biblical passages. These Scriptures will therefore be re-examined in light of their appropriate historical and cultural/linguistic origins. Much of the information in this book is based on the cultural origins and ideologies of Judaism and Christianity, but this does not limit the value of this information to those particular faiths. The principles that will be drawn out are universal and therefore can also be applied by those from other religious backgrounds or those who do not belong to a particular religion.

This book also treads where many books of faith do not dare to go in the discussion of divorce and issues surrounding it. It is like the couple who will not go out and buy life insurance or make a will because they feel that, once they do, something bad will happen to them. The author believes that the ideal plan for humanity as set down by God is for a life-long relationship of love and commitment. If each partner fulfilled that obligation of mutual love and respect, then there would be no need for a book such as this. However, the reality is that many individuals are subjected to oppression and all types of abuse, and bringing that reality to the surface and confronting it is long overdue. *That* is why this book was written—not to discard the ideal but to offer insight when the ideal has already been willfully violated or discarded by one or both partners.

The author also acknowledges that not all communities or individuals of faith condemn women who have escaped abusive situations; in fact, there are many who help them. The author is also not unaware of the fact that women can also be instigators of marital oppression. However, traditionally and throughout history men have had both civil law—and especially religious power—behind them. Women have not. That is why this book focuses on the plight of women.

It is my prayer that the insights within these pages will help free those who have suffered in these situations.

Part One

THE HISTORY

HOW DID I GET MYSELF INTO THIS MESS?

I remember the situation like it was yesterday. There I was, in my early twenties, in an apartment where the only food on hand was white sugar and tea. I had quit work because I'd recently given birth. I was in a foreign country far away from my own family. I had married a man I had become absolutely infatuated with because he had been so attentive towards me. Yet only months into the marriage I faced the sick realization that the image he'd portrayed to me had been completely deceptive. No longer was he the charming and gracious smooth-talker that had hypnotized me—he was a compulsive gambler who only spoke deceit and lies. Looking back, I see how vulnerable and stupid I was, wholeheartedly swallowing the lies, excuses, and stories he fed me.

I'd been quite independent while I was working and earning my own money, but now that I depended on his support I began asking questions about where the money was going and why the bills weren't paid. Suddenly his suave, debonair mannerisms turned ugly. All was well as long as I accepted his excuses, but when I pointed out holes in his stories, his kind face turned ruthless and angry. "What you don't know can't hurt you," he would say. I finally came to realize what that meant. If I was to be questioned about his activities by others, my naiveté might spare me. The more I uncovered, the more aggressive he became.

Despite what I began to uncover, I still believed he loved me. The truth eventually sank in. One day as we stood waiting for the bus, I questioned something he had said. This angered him, and he raised his hand to slap me, even though I was holding the baby and her face was next to mine. I heard gasps from some of the people standing nearby. Some darted their eyes away in embarrassment for me, but there were others, especially older women, who frowned and scowled out their disgust—not only at my husband but also at me. It was as if they were saying, "How can you take that?"

Indeed, how could I take it? Because I was convinced I had to. I had been raised in a Christian denomination that teaches that divorce is a sin, period. My father especially was quite religious. How could I even begin to explain to my parents that I wanted to leave this marriage, forcing them to face more disappointment and shame by having yet another divorce tagged onto the family name? Besides, I knew well the familiar response programmed into the minds of countless other women who found themselves in similar situations: "You made your bed, now sleep in it." I was so convinced that I was obligated to remain in that situation that only fear for my daughter's safety eventually forced me to even consider leaving. In fact, I clearly remember thinking that if it had only been me, if I hadn't had this baby, I would have stayed.

I sincerely believed that I should endure the abuse rather than break the vows of marriage, but now I faced a conflict with those beliefs. I could never, ever, put my baby in danger. It was her existence that began to change my thinking about staying in that relationship. Realizing that my husband was involved in some underhanded dealings, I became aware of the certain possibility that angry and vengeful men could at any moment bust down the door and break the legs of my baby girl in order to teach her father a lesson.

My suspicions were confirmed when one day someone pounded on the door and shouted, "Police!" I have never seen anyone head for an open window so fast. Suddenly the door burst open, followed by laughter. It was only some of his friends playing a trick, but I'll never forget the look on his face or the terror in my heart as both of us realized that I now knew more than I should. It was at that point I decided I had to leave.

I didn't dare whisper even a hint that I was entertaining the idea. I knew inside that he would take our daughter away one day and disappear. If he did that, I would never see her again. You see, part of the threat came from his cultural background, which included a man's "right" to keep his wife in line not only through abuse but also by threatening to take her children away from her forever.

The other thing that convinced me, and even granted me the freedom to leave, was the recurrence of a specific dream. These dreams were strong and felt very real. In them I was standing on one side of a large body of water, wanting to cross over to the opposite bank where my family stood, smiling and waving at me. My side of the water was murky and full of filth and snakes. Yet every successive dream took me in a boat closer to the other side, and the nearer I got to that other shoreline the clearer and cleaner the water became. I took this as a sign that, not only was God not angry with me for considering abandoning the marriage, He was telling me I had to.

I consider the circumstances that led me back to safety in my home country to have been divinely guided. Yet even once safely back in my own country across the ocean, I remained so terrified of being tracked down that I would examine the snow beneath my bedroom window every morning for footprints, even though my husband had never been to my country and didn't know where to find me. That terrorizing feeling remained with me for a long time, even after remarrying and having other children years later.

So why am I telling you this? It is a classic example of how and why women get themselves into abusive relationships and marriages, what makes them even consider staying, and how difficult it is to get out. It encompasses every self-accusing lie they have believed about themselves, lies which are continually reinforced by their partner's words and actions. These ideas usually stem from their upbringing, and although many originate from religious sources, others come from society in general. The important thing to remember is that all of these ideas have collectively and directly affected the treatment of women in general, and more specifically, determined their position in situations such as marriage and divorce.

Countless women endure neglect and abuse because they have been indoctrinated to believe that this is their destiny as women and it is the right of a man to control and punish them. As a result, many women never discover who they really are and everything they were meant to be. At the end of my story, I finally came to realize that it is *never* the will of God for women to endure neglect and abuse—especially from the very ones to whom they look for love and protection. It is *never* God's will to put up with evil that deflates you and makes you feel like you are nothing. In fact, one of the most difficult things I had to truly come to believe is that I am worthy of love, and as a human being I can and should expect it. So should you.

WOMEN IN THE ANCIENT WORLD

The treatment of women is directly related to the values others assign to them. Many women accept these values and, as a result, tolerate mistreatment. So how are these values determined, and what effect does it have on females worldwide?

An individual's place in society is determined by a number of factors. This includes one's biological sex and its assigned roles (which we will refer to as gender), as well as wealth, ethnicity, and age. Gender, however, is by far the strongest determinant. For example, women from wealthy families may be spared the sufferings of poverty, but their wealth does not guarantee personal freedom. In many places of the world, even wealthy women do not have the same civil rights as men in terms of how they may dress, with whom they may interact, or where they may go. In fact, in some cases women are not allowed to go out unescorted. Gender also outweighs ethnicity in terms of treatment. While visible minorities often suffer discrimination from those outside their cultural group, women from within these groups suffer further mistreatment from male members of their own culture simply because they are female. In terms of age, many societies to this day still place higher value on women of child-bearing age or those who have already borne children, especially sons. Therefore, while wealth, ethnicity, or age may affect the degree of one's status or position in society, gender is by far the strongest factor. Globally and traditionally, the female gender has occupied the bottom rung of the ladder.

While some societies have developed laws to better protect and promote females, this has not eliminated a prevailing world-wide mindset that keeps them oppressed. These attitudes are often cultivated within traditional faith teachings, yet the roots of these ideas go back much farther and penetrate much deeper. In fact, it has permeated the globe so deeply that we cannot blame only institutionalized religion.

THE IMAGE OF WOMAN: SEXUAL GODDESS OR VULNERABLE VIRGIN
Throughout history women have been valued through two basic yet fundamentally opposite qualities: the fertile mother, strong and powerful; and the pure, unadulterated virgin in need of protection. This is not to say that all women fall into one or the other of these categories, but rather, that *the perceived value* of these characteristics has played a major role in determining how women are viewed and treated in the societies in which they live.

From earliest times, long before what we consider to be traditional religion was developed, women were seen as embodying the very forces of fertility and life. It is speculated that these ideas originated as people observed how uniquely biologically equipped a woman was to bring forth new life out of her own body. Fertility and the giving of life have always been regarded as the most potent of forces in the universe, and therefore the female body became venerated for its power. This was eventually expressed in the worship of the Mother Goddess figure. Since this power was recognized as being directly related to sexual intercourse, both became intrinsically linked. This is represented throughout ancient history by various artifacts, including clay fertility goddess figures with obviously enlarged breasts and genitalia, and goddess statues—sometimes multi-breasted—whose ritual worship was often characterized by sexual indulgence and orgies. Since the earth, like women, brings forth life, the female element also became associated with earth, nature, and all of its forces. It also meant that those who usually control the resources of the earth—men—were at the mercy of the female element. In other words, Mother could just as easily destroy a harvest as bring it forth; she could just as easily and mercilessly destroy life as produce it. For this reason she is often depicted as having a dualistic nature—one productive, one destructive—as represented, for example, in the Hindu goddesses Durva and Kali.

Since the power of the female element could lead to destruction, and since this power was activated through the sexual act, it was eventually concluded that female sexuality is potentially dangerous. This was responded to in at least two ways: either this force had to be appeased or it had to be squelched. In ancient times men would visit fertility temples and offer sacrifices to the representative goddess in order to appease any potential destruction she could cause and to seek reproductive favor either for their wives or their crops and livestock. In most cases, part of the ritual involved having sexual intercourse with female temple prostitutes who were thought to be representatives of the goddess herself.

The other response to the potential danger of female power was to squelch it or keep it under control. This mindset has carried over throughout the ages and still very much exists to this day. According to this belief, attractive women—or those who exhibit qualities of strength such as confidence or intelligence—are presumed to also possess strong sexual power. As such, a strong or beautiful female is considered to be a threat not only to men but to society in general. In Islam this is referred to as *fitna* or social disorder. Men may become overpowered by this force and commit lewd or even violently sexual acts; however, if they do it is not really their fault since they are unable to resist the innate power of the female. In order to keep society safe from this potentially destructive power, it is necessary to control female beauty, and especially female sexuality. As a result, women are segregated and hidden, not so much to protect them from men but primarily to protect men from women.[1]

Although this mindset appears to be especially dominant in Islamic society, it also exists within certain factions or denominations of other religious communities, especially those of an extreme orthodox nature. This is why there are differences within groups belonging to the same religion, since not all agree with this viewpoint. If that is the case, this tells us that religion itself per se is not the main culprit.

In fact, this mindset exists beyond so-called religious frameworks. I have met women who have been abusively dominated by men simply because he is the male and she is the female—and these people were not "religious." This attitude has also manifested itself in our courts, where female victims of rape have been accused of "asking for it."

Ironically, families or societies that are dominated by this mindset sometimes appear to elevate the matriarch or mother of the family; however, this is often based on fear and not on ideas of male/female or parental equality. For example, sons are doted upon simply because they are male, and since males must not show weakness, any so-called respect or desire to please their mother often stems from a personal fear that she will see them as weak or sinful. For this reason the patriarch must also portray an image of absolute control, often becoming extremely domineering, even cruel, in order to maintain that image.

A common response to fear is to manipulate, and therefore family or group members with these dynamics are in a constant power struggle with each other. The matriarch, for example, may be extremely manipulative and domineering towards those under her, the children, since this is the only area in her life where she feels she has any control or power. Daughters-in-law are often especially targeted since they are the ones with potential to "dethrone" her either by replacing her as the center of the son's affections, or by bringing forth sons themselves. The more this mindset is embedded within a family or culture, the greater the fear of female power and subsequent attempts to control women, especially those who exhibit charisma through beauty, intelligence, or independence.

The second perceived ideal quality in women is that of the pure virgin—pure not only in body but also in mind. Unfortunately, when this viewpoint is perverted, women, especially virgins, are presumed to be weak and sometimes even lower in intellectual and spiritual ability than men. Individuals or groups who adhere to this perversion are protective of their virgins to the extreme of covering them or restricting their movements and contacts within the rest of society. Here, men also have the monopoly on decision-making within the framework of relationship. We see this particularly manifested in societies that are ruled by a dominant male figure and that marry off child brides in order to "protect" them from greater society. In this system, a woman makes all the sacrifices in the relationship while the will of the male is central.

As with the Mother Goddess image, this viewpoint is also not confined to mainstream religion, although both greatly use it. While the driving force behind the Mother Goddess image is a fear of female power, the force behind the Virgin image is the belief that females are innately inferior to males. Both, however, have this in common—an underlying despising of the female gender. In fact, we often see characteristics of both views operating together in society.

Here's why.

In pre-history and early history these two elements—the powerful mother and the innocent virgin—became intermingled. Their combination created the singularly most powerful and feared female entity in the universe: the Mother/Virgin goddess. The Mother/Virgin goddess is historically depicted with a male god-infant, with pre-eminence given to the power of the Mother. So widespread was this form of worship in ancient times that early Catholic missionaries were amazed to find existing statues of "Mary and Jesus" in parts of the world that far pre-dated Christianity. This combination is characterized by a pressure on men to constantly project an image of strength and virility because of an internal fear of female power on the one hand and an underlying sense of male entitlement on the other.

Wherever this exists, be it in secular or religious settings, the results are disastrous. All sorts of vile abuses and oppressions occur against females, ranging from denying them the basics of human survival—food, shelter and protection—to the justification of beatings. It also often results in some form of sexual depravity toward girls and women: sexual exploitation, incest, or rape. Females who live within this framework eventually become so devalued in their own minds that many allow boyfriends and men in general to sexually use them as they please. After all, what is there left to protect? This stretches some into a life of prostitution. On the other extreme are cases where families actually sell their young daughters into human trafficking rings to become sex slaves.

Although the Mother/Virgin goddess is a female image, the spirit behind it is actually hostile to her. It triggers fear of female power, which in turn justifies the "need" for males to control and abuse females, especially once they reach womanhood. Although this belief and the spirit behind it is traceable to the earliest of human history, we see it continually pops up throughout time, even among civilizations that claimed to be "progressing."

Life for Women in Ancient Rome

Some of the greatest influences within human history emerged from ancient Greece and Rome. We still see the marks of these civilizations in our modern world in art, education, and politics, all considered to be progressive and positive developments. Yet other influences, just as strong but no so positive, were also handed down—including an age-old negative attitude toward women.

The Romans were great admirers of the ancient Greeks, borrowing many of their cultural ideas. In fact, one of the reasons why Rome became so powerful and lasted so long was its ability to absorb well-selected cultural and religious elements of the people groups it conquered, provided that these did not conflict with or contradict Roman principle and life. This enabled them to maintain control, since the masses were less likely to revolt if they were allowed to retain some of their own cultural identity. Therefore, although Rome did have a strong military presence, it dominated more through ideological influence than by force.

One of the main elements Rome absorbed was the Mother/Virgin cults. The Great Mother Cybele was especially esteemed in Roman society, although her veneration, again, was based more on a healthy respect for her potential to destroy, especially men. Cybele myths describe how her power and anger could cause men to go mad and castrate themselves. Cybele cultic priests in Rome were, in fact, castrated. While this fear resulted in veneration for the goddess, for the ordinary human female it meant being controlled in everyday life. In response to this repression, secretive groups were formed within goddess worship circles, which emphasized the power of the female element to the benefit of its female members. This benefit did not transcend into everyday life but was confined to ritualistic worship. These groups, referred to as mystery cults because of their secretiveness, considered women to be intuitively and even spiritually superior to men, and as a result they were particularly attractive to women. Their rituals allowed them freedom of personal expression, unrestricted from male domination. It is no wonder that they appealed to women, since in both ancient Greece and Rome women had little respect or rights.

According to Roman law, for example, a man literally owned his wife and children to the point that he had the right to put them to death for any reason that he deemed justifiable. While wealthy women held more status than their poor counterparts, they were still basically male property. Daughters from influential families were usually married off as a means of securing political alliances and security for the family, in particular for the men. For most of Rome's history only men had the right to initiate divorce—for any reason—and usually did so in order to improve their political career or social station by then remarrying a woman with greater family influence and wealth. The wealthy woman was therefore valued more as a commodity than an individual.

Marriages in the classical ancient worlds of Greece and Rome were, for the most part, emotionless, not based on love or even sexual gratification, at least for the woman. Mistresses and lovers took care of that, and it was commonplace for married men especially to indulge in sexual orgies. A good wife in classical times minded her own business, kept a well-run home and, most importantly, dared not demand respect or emotional fulfillment from her husband.

Yet, in time, another culture conquered by ancient Rome infiltrated everyday life which, like the mystery cults, also appealed to women. But contrary to popular belief, this one gave them rights.

WOMEN & EARLY JUDAISM

THE "OTHER" WAY OF LIFE IN ANCIENT ROME

Judaism and the culture behind it stood out to the ancient Romans not only as odd but downright irritating. This was for a number of reasons. First, Jews resisted the idea of worshipping anyone or anything (including Caesar) other than the Great God of Heaven. They had weird ritualistic and eating habits, and they actively proselytized or sought converts. What was particularly annoying and, as mentioned earlier, found to be surprising to many, is that their way of life was particularly appealing to women. While it is largely believed that ancient Judaism had a low opinion of women, when we dig deeper into the roots and the cultural settings of the time, we find that the status and role of women within Judaism may not have been as oppressive as previously thought. Dr. J. H. Hertz, in the commentaries of the *Pentateuch and Haftorahs*, writes:

> *It is astonishing to note the amount of hostile misrepresentation that exists in regard to woman's position in Bible times. "The relation of the wife to the husband was, to all intents and purposes, that of a slave to her master," are the words of a writer in the* Encyclopaedia of Religion and Ethics. *That this judgment is radically false may be proved from hundreds of instances throughout Scripture."*[2]

Historian Louis Feldman states that women were drawn as converts to Judaism probably due to the "relatively more elevated and respected position of women in the Jewish community."[3] It should also be noted here that early Christianity began as a Judaic sect and, for approximately the first century of its existence, its practices were fully based on Judaism and therefore also appealed to women. This attraction is documented as late as the fourth century. By that time Christianity had pulled away from its Judaic roots and had adopted a gender-restrictive attitude toward women (discussed in detail later). This attraction bothered the church authority of the time so much that they issued decrees against it. For example, Apostolic Canons 69 and 37 dating from the mid-fourth century forbid the participation of Christians in Jewish festivals, *and in particular the women*, since they were the ones who tended to continue these practices (italics mine for emphasis). Chrysostom in *Adversus Judaeos* 2.3.860 charges "Christian husbands with the responsibility of *keeping wives from going to the synagogues.*"[4]

This is not to say that Jewish women were always treated fairly. As in all religions, there are always those who take a harsher stance. However, our interest is in the "official" position of women within Judaism at the time and not the personal opinions of separate individuals. For example, did Judaism provide women with legal or civic recourse if they were oppressed or mistreated?

In Jewish history there have been both high and low points, but the overall treatment of women within Judaic culture appears to have been better than in non-Judaic societies. Author and lecturer of ancient history James W. Fleming affirms that up to the second century B.C./B.C.E. Jewish women were not only highly esteemed but even held responsible positions of authority.[5] I will refer to this as the "biblical" period, the time referred to in general by Christians as the Old Testament.

An example of this is found in the Proverbs 31:10–31 description of a woman who is more than just a housewife; she runs the household economy and is an astute businesswoman (vv. 14, 18, 24). She does not hand over her profits to her husband but keeps them for reinvestment of her choosing (vv. 16, 31). Her husband is esteemed by virtue of his wife, not the opposite. Some have argued that since this woman merely reinvests her efforts and profits back into the home, she is still confined to the home. That conclusion, however, is arrived at when we interpret this passage from our modern viewpoint of economy; previous to the Industrial Revolution of the West and still in many parts of the world today, home-based production was the center of economy, with women acting as key producers and distributors. We therefore need to analyze the Proverbs 31 woman in the context of her own time and societal economy.

In ancient Israel, the home was the foothold of family wealth and production. Although property was under the man's name, it was technically the family he came from and not him personally, per se, who owned it. In our economy of private ownership this is hard for us to understand. Ownership of property was passed from generation to generation usually via the firstborn son as a means of security for the wife and any minor children should her husband predecease her, which he usually did.

This understanding of ownership is the basis for many Israelite traditions, such as naming a firstborn son after a forefather. The name was "proof" of family affiliation and hence, property rights. Upon the father's death, the firstborn inherited not only the property but also the responsibility to look after his widowed mother and any dependent siblings, family members, and servants. The tradition of the younger, unmarried brother marrying his older brother's widow and naming their firstborn son after his brother (levirate marriage) was founded on this principle. This guaranteed the property would remain in the family so that widows and orphans would not be left destitute.

Thus, the ancient Israelite system was meant to safeguard and protect women and their children against homelessness and, therefore, poverty. If there were no sons, then the daughters inherited the property, as seen in the case of the daughters of Zelophehad recorded in the book of Numbers Chapter 27. The wording in the text reinforces the fact that the daughters' rights to the property were secured by the father's, or family name (vv. 4–11).

Jewish law also assigned equal value to both males and females. In Exodus 21:31 it states that compensation for the loss of either a male or female child must be the same. The Ten Commandments also direct us to honor both father *and* mother (Exodus 20:12). Some point out that the redemptive value of a son was higher than for a daughter. This, however, was directly linked to the weightier role of spiritual responsibility imposed on males, something we will discuss in greater detail further on. In other words, assigned role differences pertaining to gender in the Bible were based on responsibility rather than personal value. This is important because it tells us that the original precedent to be followed is *not to equate an individual's personal value with their role or function in society*. In fact, the Bible instructs that extra consideration be given to the potentially vulnerable (sometimes awkwardly translated as "weaker") members of society, especially women and children.

So what about the seemingly unequal nature of the roles between men and women in Scripture? Many traditionally-accepted interpretations of these teachings stem from religious authorities and scholars who wittingly or unwittingly applied their own personal or cultural standards rather than the proper historical and Judaic context. First of all, we must remember that roles were based on *physical ability, circumstantial flexibility,* and *social/spiritual responsibility.* In other words, physical strength, dictation of time, and relationship-related obligations were more likely to serve as hindrances to participation rather than simply one's gender, which many assume to be the only basis for restriction. Notwithstanding these hindrances, equality exists.

One such example is the role of the prophet. Contrary to popular belief, a prophet was not simply a foreteller of the future, although predictions of possible consequences were at times tied in with a prophet's message. It was more the job of the prophet to reveal the will of God through Scripture and example and to urge individuals to right action. The office and authority of a prophet were accepted as being from God Himself and required knowledge of His Word. Interestingly, prophetesses (female prophets) were equally recognized in ancient Israel, as in the cases of Deborah and Huldah. Deborah was also a Judge, another position of authority that included the rendering of judicial decisions over both men and women. Not only did the men of their times not question their authority, they sought out their wisdom. In fact, although Huldah was a contemporary of the great prophet Jeremiah, the priest Hilkiah sought out her counsel (2 Kings 22:14; 2 Chronicles 34:22).

Speaking of priests, the fact that there were no female priests in the Old Testament is often used to justify the exclusion of women from spiritual service in some religious circles today. The underlying insinuation is that women are spiritually incapable or inferior. This, however, is a weak argument and one that is based on an ignorance of the difference between the function of the Old Testament priesthood and modern day orders.

The role of the priest in the Old Testament had less to do with spiritual or male superiority than it did with the physical and practical requirements of the job. First of all, the priest was no more spiritual than the rest of the people because both were equally accountable to God. Remember also that the priesthood excluded most males. It was an inherited tribal position passed down within families, which made it easier to instill a proper mindset and training within upcoming generations. Moreover, one also had to be free from any mental or physical impediments. Priests were also not allowed to own their own property and were totally supported by the rest of Israelite society. This stands to reason, since it would have been impossible for them to labor full hours as a priest and work at a trade at the same time in order to support their family. This brings us to the main reason women could not be priests. It would have been difficult, if not impossible both physically and time-wise, for women as natural bearers of children to act as priests. Not only was it a morning to evening full-time position it also required the continuous lifting, slaughtering, and dismembering of oxen, sheep, and other animals. Therefore, gender itself was not so much the issue in determining priesthood as which factors best empowered an individual to fulfill that role.

Judaism still enacts these principles of either obligation or exemption in regards to the keeping of *mitzvot* (commandments) by categorizing them as either "negative" or "positive." Positive commandments, for example, are ruled by time, and therefore, women are not obligated to keep these as are men. Consequently, Jewish men have always had a weightier role of responsibility assigned to them in terms of time-dictated and physical obligations.

Although they could not be priests, women did serve at the entrance of the Tent of Meeting.[6] Moreover, their restriction from the priesthood itself did not mean that they had no essential role in the spiritual well-being of Israelite society. While the priesthood represented the nation and community in general before God, it was the women who were responsible for the maintenance of worship and ritual in the home. In Judaism, the home was and still is considered to be the epicenter of spiritual strength and instruction, so much so that it is often described in Jewish texts as the "altar." In that way one could say that women held their own "priestly" position, one that was paramount to their cultural survival. Hertzberg comments that the Jewish *people*, not just men, were bound by the covenant with God "...to the task of being a corporate priesthood."[7] Both genders were expected to obey the Law, and each individual was held personally accountable for their own sin. Although carried out in different contexts and through different duties, the roles of men and women were, and still are, equally important to Judaic culture.

Around the end of "biblical" times, however, that is, about the time of the second century, we do see a decline in the elevated status of Jewish women. There is no solid evidence as to why this happened, but it appears that Jewish spiritual and cultural leadership began to absorb the influences of the classical ancient world, especially the Greeks. As mentioned earlier, although Rome was in charge, Greek influence pervaded society. For example, by the time of Jesus of Nazareth, the main language both written and spoken was Koine Greek. This next period in Judaism, following the "biblical" age, is known as the Talmudic period.[8]

Ancient Greece was repressive to its women. From the Archaic to the Hellenic ages, Greek women had no personal status from a legal or civic position. In general, Greek wives were normally kept secluded, rarely spoke to their husbands, and were expected to be hardworking, loyal, and obedient. It was only during the later Hellenistic period that women began to have any autonomy, but like the Romans, it was the privileged, wealthy women who had more status. Overall, Greek society was stringently male-dominated . . . and very much admired and imitated.

Stephen B. Clark outlines evidence for this decrease in female respect within rabbinical thinking that appears to be synonymous with the adoption of Greek ideas, including an increasing separation of women from men in public life.[9] However, nothing can be proven with certainty. Regardless of the reasons, it is assumed that by and around the time of Jesus of Nazareth and afterward, the status of Jewish women in the eyes of Jewish religious leadership was becoming inferior to that of their biblical predecessors.

Although Jewish women lost some status during this time, they were still officially better off compared to women in other cultures.

For example, they had certain legal rights such as the protection of the *ketubah* or marriage contract, which is still used today. According to Dr. J. H. Hertz, the ketubah was introduced as protocol in Jewish life *as early as the first pre-Christian century* by Simeon ben Shetach and was deliberately designed to protect the wife in the event of her becoming widowed or divorced (italics mine for emphasis).[10]

Obviously, there had to be justifiable reason to introduce such an important document into everyday culture, and I believe the reason was the very thing just discussed—an increase in disrespect toward women, which threatened their overall welfare. So while negative influences from the outside were being introduced into Judaic thinking by some leaders, others worked to counterbalance this threat by introducing protective documents such as the ketubah. We will be discussing the role of the ketubah and another document common in Judaism, the *get* or bill of divorcement, in greater detail in upcoming chapters on marriage and divorce. Not only did the ketubah make it costly for Jewish men to dump their wives, it was originally designed to make men accountable for how they treated them.

It appears, then, that overall, Judaism has been concerned for the welfare of its women, especially when compared to other cultures. As in all things, there were exceptions; however, one key difference is the attempt to counterbalance these negative influences. This is important to remember, especially as we go into our next chapter, which discusses the status and treatment of women in another setting—Christianity. Christianity is somewhat unique in that, unlike most mainstream religions, it has moved away from its original source and character, especially in regards to women. As we trace these changes throughout its history, it will become evident just where those influences came from and to what degree they have now infiltrated our own, modern thinking.

WOMEN & EARLY CHRISTIANITY
The Religion You Thought You Knew

From its inception in the first century until the demise of Rome toward the end of the fifth century Christianity underwent many changes, and the shifting in the status of women within the church can be seen as synonymous with those changes.

So far we have looked at the life of non-Jewish women in ancient times up to and including life in the Roman Empire just prior to and during the establishment of Christianity, and we have noted the status and function of women in Judaism during this same period. It is important here to remember that Christianity began as a Jewish sect, because the Judaic attitude toward women played a direct role in earliest Christianity.

Jesus' disciples consisted of women as well as men, both poor and rich.[11] A close examination of the Gospels reveals the Jewish cultural respect for women. Initially, earliest Christianity, being a Jewish sect, retained these elements; that is, men and women had different roles but were considered equals, and husbands as household heads were obligated to greater responsibility and servitude to the wife. Although many individuals see Jesus as regarding women as equals, the rest of the New Testament, especially the Pauline letters, has traditionally been accused of being primarily responsible for lowering the position of women.

This viewpoint has recently begun to be challenged by some scholars as Scriptures are re-examined in their Jewish cultural and historical contexts. Obviously, there are difficult passages that seem to not only restrict women's role in the church but also the home. Stendahl comments that when these difficulties result in diametrically opposite conclusions, the problem is usually that of different principles of application and interpretation.[12] Further study usually reveals a simple cultural explanation that has no direct bearing on status or role or has been wrongfully interpreted according to a different culture or time.

One such example is found in Paul's first letter to Timothy (2:14–15), usually translated as "...woman will be saved through bearing children, if she continues in faith." This statement very much appears to back up society's attitude that a woman's role is in the kitchen, barefoot and pregnant. However, the literal interpretation can be read as "she will be saved by the birth of the child," which many believe is actually a reference to the promise made in Genesis Chapter 3 of the woman and her seed, the Messiah. The church teaches that one is saved by faith in that Child.[13] Moreover, if woman's redemption is achieved only through motherhood, what about those who are unable to or by choice have no children?

In the time of the original apostles and the Apostolic Fathers, women actually held important positions of leadership. One example is found in Paul's reference to Phoebe in Romans 16:1–2. Although usually translated "deaconess," the original Greek word in this text was written in the masculine form.[14] The word "deacon" was an official church function comprising ministerial duties. Paul also mentions many other women in the greetings and closings of his various letters, and he often refers to them as "co-worker" or "fellow laborer"—terms of equality.

Most of these women are presumed to be single, but at least two couples are also mentioned which have interesting stories behind them. Dr. Fleming uses them to illustrate the esteemed status of women in the early church. First, there are Priscilla and Aquila (Romans 16:3–5), first mentioned in Acts 18:2 where Paul meets them in Corinth and addressed again in the letter to the Ephesians. They are both recognized as teachers as well as apostles, positions which have traditionally become restricted to men. In fact, both Priscilla and Aquila taught Apollos, and both traveled with Paul on his journey to the church in Syria (Acts 18). Paul not only writes their names interchangeably in the salutations of his various letters, but in his letters to the Romans he places Priscilla before Aquila. Since order of placement was usually indicative of importance or authority, this means that Paul not only regarded them as equals in the ministry and as individuals, but there is even a possibility that Priscilla had a more esteemed position among the Roman church.

The case of Andronicus and Junias in the last chapter of Romans is even more interesting. Dr. Fleming refers to a traceable change in the spelling of the name Junias (fem.) to that of Junia (masc.) in the 1300's, reputed to have been done by a monk who had difficulties reconciling the fact that Paul called both of them apostles! The change still exists in some translations. Clark affirms, as do other sources, that both men and women were teachers and apostles in the early church and that Paul had worked with many of them.[15]

During the age of the Apostolic Fathers (late first century, beginning of second century) the church was in constant struggle against the infiltration of all types of teachings that the Christian leaders felt threatened their doctrine. Some of the teachers of these ideas made claims that they received their teachings from the apostles themselves or were known to them. The church, therefore, eventually found it necessary to establish apostolic succession as a means of stability against what they saw as heresy. This ended up being one of the main factors denigrating the status and role of women in the church.[16] Women were pushed out of leadership positions on the pretexts that the Twelve chosen by Jesus were all males and women did not serve as priests in the time of the Old Testament (see our discussion on this in the previous section).

The other factor that weakened the value and position of women in the church was, ironically, the embracing of an outside ideology into the very structure of Christianity—asceticism. Asceticism was present in many Gnostic teachings and popular in Greek thinking. One of its fundamental beliefs was that matter or flesh, being imperfect and therefore evil, must be overcome. Since sexual desire was seen as one of the strongest passions of the flesh, the best way to spiritual perfection was through celibacy. As a result, that same old idea that the female gender should be regarded as a threat to male spiritual purity because men were considered to be easily attracted to and seduced by female beauty began to establish itself in the heart of Christian doctrine. This mindset probably found its opening through the influence of the many Roman and Greek converts being added to the new faith. At that time the mystery cults were still active, and therefore the emerging church authority used the cults' ritual practices as "proof" of the inherent dangers of the female gender.[17]

As formerly discussed, the inequality of women usually arises from two basic premises: that they are dangerous, sexual creatures who, if not guarded, can cause the downfall of man; or that they are weak and can only survive under the protection of a dominant male. We can trace the increasing influence of this spirit within the church with each passing century as it discarded its Judaic roots and adopted more and more the mindset of those who were converting. So on one extreme there was the deceptive Eve (Mother), who overpowered man and successfully lured him into partaking of the forbidden fruit (which many presumed to be sex), while on the other there was the chaste Virgin Mary, whose status went from a humble and merely human handmaiden of the Lord in early Christianity to that of goddess[1] status in the fifth century.[18]

As this dualistic approach increased, leadership positions were taken away from married women (who, of course, were presumed to be sexually active) and entrusted only to celibate widows and virgins. As the ascetic lifestyle took hold in regular Christian life, separate monasteries and nunneries for men and women were developed.

The time of the Early Fathers (second to third centuries) is marked by individuals such as Clement of Alexandria and Tertullian. Both had been strongly influenced by teachings of celibacy and asceticism, and both had a double standard of ethics regarding women and marriage. For example, while Tertullian refers to marriage as a blissful union in which couples teach each other, he also considered it a lesser evil. Clement did not think marriage was "natural," and it was the "disease of the body" (sexual desire) that necessitated it. Both saw procreation as the only true purpose of marriage, ignoring the innate human need for intimacy and companionship. In fact, Tertullian referred to second marriages as adulterous regardless of the circumstances which led up to them, a view he based on the premise of reunion after death.[19] He obviously did not regard Jesus' statement that in the resurrection no one is bound by marriage (Matthew 22:30). But he truly reveals his dualistic attitude in his description of women as the deceitful Eve:

> *You are the devil's gateway: you are the unsealer of that (forbidden tree); you are the first deserter of the divine law; you are she who persuaded him whom the devil was not valiant enough to attack. You destroyed God's image, man. On account of your desert -- that is, death, even the son of God had to die. Why adorn yourself? All of the luxury of feminine dress is the baggage of women in her condemned and dead estate.*[20]

---

[1] Some may take issue with this wording, but the bowing down to statues of Mary and praying to her were practices that would have been recognized by the ancient public as goddess worship.

Despite this negative viewpoint of the female gender in general, it had been necessary to keep women in the position of deaconess in order to minister to other women, such as for the anointing and baptizing of female adherents. By the time of the Late Fathers, however, a major shift had also occurred in the nature of the deaconess's office. It was now only widows, fifty years and older, and virgins, forty years old and over, who were allowed this ministry, since the office of deaconess was now directly linked with the maintenance of chastity.

According to a canon of the Council of Chalcedon, if a deaconess (widow or virgin) did decide to marry, her choice was seen as a despising of God's grace, and she was therefore "anathematized and the man united to her." The marriage was considered adulterous (since the woman was considered to be "married" to Christ), and therefore, as Basil writes in his Canon on "Fallen" Virgins, the marriage "must by all means be dissolved."[21] Despite the apostle Paul's statement that it is not a sin for such people to marry, his counsel went unheeded and was replaced by the will of the Church Fathers (see 1 Corinthians 7:28). Paul's only discouragement against marriage is that it divides one's interests, not because it is a betrayal to the Lord or a sin. In fact, he actually counsels young widows to marry, and only those sixty years and older were eligible to be put on the "widows list" (for the purpose of church support) since there was still a likelihood that they might marry before then (1 Timothy 5:9, 14).

Eventually not even widows could be ordained. The *Canons of Hippolytus,* (336 and 340 A.D.; Canons 9 and 11) declare that, according to apostolic precept, *no women* should be ordained in an official church position and that "female presidents" are *no longer* to be appointed but are to serve only in the capacity of prayer, fasting, and the care of the sick (italic emphasis mine).[22] The fact that these Canons were alterations to former practices is proof of female leadership in the early church.

As stated before, power over another is realized not by personal opinion but by official or active legislation. The church that existed just prior to the demise of Rome not only restricted women's roles in religious life but also their personal lives. Not only did church canon dictate whether or not they could marry, or when, or whom, it began imposing rules on the personal lives of those who were already married. Although admitting that Jesus allowed for divorce from an unfaithful spouse for either man or woman (Matthew 5: 32), Basil writes that the church's custom now "does not hold so . . . but enjoins that adulterous and promiscuous husbands be retained by their wives," but if it is the wife who strays, the husband must "send away from his home a defiled wife."[23] Basil also declares that guilt will be attached to the woman who divorces her husband even if she "was beaten and refused to submit to this treatment, she ought to have endured it rather than be separated from her husband."

The further along the church moved into history, the further it moved away from the original perspective that women are to be esteemed by their husbands. As a result, the time of the Late Fathers did not see even marital unfaithfulness and beatings as justifiable reasons for a woman to leave her husband. In Basil's own admission, "...we find a greater strictness in regard to women."[24] By the time Rome came to be known as the Christian Empire, it was also dictating how women should dress. According to Cyprian, virgins (unmarried women) had no business wearing ornaments or garments that were attractive since such allurements were considered "not fitting for any but prostitutes and immodest women."

The humble Jewish sect that Christianity began as, and which regarded its women with honor had, by turning its back on its roots and adopting beliefs from the prevailing culture, gradually evolved into both a religious and political monster that now not only advocated but also legislated the right for men to cheat, starve, abuse, and dump their wives without support. The status and role of women had moved from that of esteemed partner both in religion and in the home to that of inferior slave, both of the official church and the husband. How ironic that the very faith that promised women freedom in the beginning ended up being the very thing that chained them all the more in the end. The saddest thing is that, to this day, many Christian denominations feel obligated to uphold those same archaic views and laws even to the point of condemning women who leave abusive and neglectful husbands for fear that, if the church does rescind, it is leaving the way of God.

To many Christians out there reading this, especially those who take offense to the last few paragraphs, remember that what you have just read is history and not mere opinion. You can look at this, then, in two ways: acknowledge the wrongful infiltrations that happened over history and make a sincere attempt to honor those original roots from which your faith arose, or remain defensively stubborn in order to blindly protect the fact of those infiltrations. I believe it is time in the earth's history for Christianity to look back to her roots and in so doing save her honor and restore her effectiveness in the world. Both Judaism and Christianity have claimed to be bringers of light to the world. If they do not act now to reconcile it will be the world's loss, especially for those whom they have originally and traditionally been called to uphold and fight for—the widow and the orphan.[2]

I want to close this chapter by clarifying definitions of the word "church". "Church" can have two meanings: it can refer to the "official" governing body that oversees a particular group; it can also simply mean the individual believers themselves. "The Church" mentioned above refers to the official governing body that evolved during the first few centuries after the time of Jesus of Nazareth and became a political as well as a religious institution. Genuine, original Christianity, of which some forms exist today, emphasizes the love of God and manifests it through serving and giving to others, as opposed to those groups who misuse the name of God to abuse and impose restrictions on others.

I also want to note that these abuses are not only found in tainted forms of Christianity but also in other religions. Unfortunately, power-seeking, selfish individuals often use religion as a means of gaining control over others. Hopefully, by the end of this book, you will be able to discern the negative elements that have infiltrated into the Christian faith and spare the good.

---

[2] It is interesting to note that the Judaic perspective regards the term "widow" as also referring to a married woman who is either abandoned or forgotten by her husband or who remains in his house and is even provided for by him yet is intimately neglected and alone, the same as a woman whose husband has died (see 2 Sam. 20: 3).

THE
COVENANT

MARRIAGE 101

What we expect of marriage today and how we traditionally tend to describe it comes down to us largely from the influence of the church. That is not to say that marriage rituals or symbolism from other sources are unimportant or are not used, but rather that marriage in mainstream western society is derived largely from Christian tradition. It is therefore essential to examine how these traditions evolved. Since the roots of Christianity derived from Judaism, we need to look at marriage from the context of both Judaic and Christian perspectives, especially in their earlier forms.

Since ancient times, according to Judaism there were three ways for a man to acquire a wife: by a symbolic handing over of money, through written guarantee, or by sexual intercourse.[25] This is not unlike many other cultures; however, marriage in Judaism was also always regarded as a *mutual* contractual agreement between both the man and the woman. In fact, as far back as biblical times a woman had to herself give consent to marry the man.[26] This may surprise many, since most of us have seen popular stories such as *Fiddler on the Roof,* where a matchmaker was used by the parents to help make the proper choice of spouse, not so different from modern-day Orthodox practices in which the young woman's parents decide whom she will marry. It must be noted, however, that as the Jews became increasingly dispersed from the Holy Land into other nations, they adopted some of the customs of those nations. Two such examples are matchmaking and the custom of inviting a rabbi to conduct the marriage ceremony. This latter practice only began in the late Middle Ages and, in the words of the author of *The Essential Talmud,* was, in fact, ironically in part an imitation of the Christian marriage ceremony.[27] Despite these added-on traditions, the basic essence of marriage in Judaism is that it is a covenantal agreement between a man and woman based on the principles of Torah, or God's Law, with the community serving as witness of their accountability to each other.

Besides being a covenant, the precepts of marriage are also assumed to have derived from Scripture. In fact, just about every Christian church bases its premise of marriage on church doctrine and traditions supposedly originating from those Scriptures. Unfortunately, the result has been a negative image of Christianity and traditional marriage and even the Bible itself, since in the Christian context the Scriptures are often interpreted to place women into a role of mute submission under the husband, even if he is abusive, an interpretation which seems to be contrary to what the heart of God should be. As mentioned earlier, I personally struggled with this contradiction, unable to reconcile the fact that a loving and merciful God would expect me or any other woman to be personally or religiously obligated to not only tolerate evil but to obey it as well.

So what about those scriptures that seem to portray women as inferior subjects within the marriage? Confusion and contradiction arise when we attempt to interpret a scripture out of its original context; therefore, it is essential that we re-examine marriage, not from the cultural and religiously-dictated presumptions that have evolved throughout the ages but from the original foundations from which the covenant and scriptures were derived. If we do not understand the true function and meaning behind covenant, we will be unable to grasp the significance of the scriptures upon which it is based, and we will continue to justify the denigration of women in marriage. Let us therefore take a look at marriage in its context as a covenantal agreement based on scriptures from Bible times.

Marriage as Covenant

The Hebrew word for covenant is *brit*, the same word used to describe the relationship between God and Abraham. According to Zodhiates, it was "a treaty, alliance of friendship, a pledge, an obligation between a monarch and his subjects, a constitution" that was accompanied by "signs, sacrifices, and a solemn oath which sealed the relationship with promises of blessings for obedience and curses for disobedience."[28]

Covenants usually involved a "greater" partner and a "lesser" partner (sometimes poorly translated as "weaker"). This does not mean that one partner had more personal value than the other but rather describes the type and degree of contributions expected from each. In other words, "greater" partners were expected to bear a greater burden of responsibility and personal sacrifice within the covenant. They were also usually the initiators of the relationship, and it is in that sense that they were also viewed as leaders.

Leaders are meant to lead, or initiate. This quality of leadership within the original biblical framework has been replaced by a prevailing attitude that leadership means having indisputable authority—and that often without accountability. The Bible, however, views leadership as a role of example and servitude. In other words, our "greatness" is directly related to how well we serve others and the type of living example we are. We see this reflected in Jesus' statement to his disciples, who had been arguing over who would be the greatest. His response was: "If anyone desires to be first, he shall be last of all and servant of all." (Mark 9:35). Peter clarifies this concept of leadership to the elders of the early church: "Shepherd the flock of God which is among you, serving as overseers, not by constraint but willingly, not for dishonest gain but eagerly, *nor as being lords over those entrusted to you, but being examples to the flock.*" (1 Peter 5:2–3) [Italics mine for emphasis].

To "lord it over" others is to have the attitude that you are superior and therefore everyone should bend to your will. According to the Bible, then, true covenantal marriage means that the husband is not superior to his wife, nor is he her owner or boss. On the contrary, as the "greater" partner in the covenant, he is obligated to lead by example. This includes not expecting his wife or family members to do anything that he himself is unwilling to do, and to consider their needs first. Yet many husbands today enter marriage expecting their wives to cater to them in much the same way they were catered to by their mothers. Let us remember that children are often catered to or given precedence of attention because of their immaturity and inability to look after themselves. However, serving a child should gradually lessen as they mature and take on further responsibility. If a husband still expects his wife to cater to him as a child is catered to, he is not worthy of the respect due to the mature and responsible. He cannot be a leader and a little boy at the same time.

As well as being the initiator or leader of the covenant, the "greater" partner was also responsible for a greater role of sacrifice. This included the duty to provide for, or cover, the other partner. According to the Scriptures, there were three basic categories of provision that a man was required to give his wife: food (Heb. *she'er*); clothing or covering (*kesut*); and marital or conjugal rights (*ona*).[29]

The first category, food, does not simply mean paying the grocery bill. From ancient times, food has been recognized and acknowledged as the source of physical health and well-being. It would therefore not be an exaggeration to synonymously use the words *nourishment* or *nurturing* with food. A husband was therefore expected to feed and nourish his wife, implying that he was responsible for her health and well being. Lack of food was a sign of poverty and therefore most likely a reflection of the husband's unreliability or incapability to properly nourish his wife.

The second provisional item is clothing. Think of what clothes do. They cover our nakedness, which in ancient times was directly associated with shame. By virtue of analogy, then, a man must never shame or humiliate his wife. Clothing also protects us from the elements and keeps us warm. Equally important, the type of clothing you wore in those days signified your status. For example, only the wealthy could afford to wear the expensive purple or blue cloth. Wide hems were also indicators of wealth and prestige. With regard to status, there is a general rule in Judaism which states that when a man takes a wife "she ascends with him and does not descend with him." In other words, a man who marries a woman from a lower social class or status must lift her up to his class or standard, but if he marries a woman of a higher class than himself, he must raise himself up to her standards. As put in *The Essential Talmud,* "he has no right to reduce her standard of living without her explicit agreement."[30] This is reflected in the Hebrew word *noseh*, used specifically to refer to a man marrying a woman. The word also means "to carry, lift up or esteem."[31] Therefore, when a man marries a woman, he is lifting her up, not abasing her; carrying her, not depending on her; and esteeming her, not belittling her. There is also a sense of humor here, for the word can also mean to bear or endure, suffer or forgive (I can hear some husbands saying "amen" to that), words directly related to the concept of sacrifice which we will be discussing in greater detail further down.

Is this not a beautiful picture of marriage? Did you ever wonder why the bride is *lifted up* during a Jewish wedding celebration? The groom is also lifted up, and why not? He has just lifted his status in the community by taking on a wife, as it is written in the Talmud, "A man without a woman is doomed to an existence without joy, without blessing, without experiencing life's true goodness, without Torah, without protection and without peace." The Bible echoes, "He who finds a wife finds a good thing, and obtains favor from the Lord" (Proverbs 18:22).

It may be easy for us to understand the concepts of provision and protection through food and clothing, but what about "marital rights"? The obvious aspect to this is intimacy. Judaism has established certain principles based on this instruction. In fact, it is very frank and specific in its discussion of sexual issues. Having been raised in a Christian environment and being exposed to Judaism later in life, this unabashed forwardness somewhat shocked me since Christianity treats the topic of sex as secretive, even taboo. The tragedy of this attitude is the effect it has had on marriage, not just among Christians themselves but among the general western culture it has infiltrated. As a result, the topic and open exploration of sex and sexual desires has been left to perverted forms such as pornography. Yet matters of sexuality and intimacy play a large role in the health of a marriage, and therefore a discussion of sex should no longer be ignored within faith circles. Unfortunately many church counselors are uneasy dealing with the nitty-gritty of the topic, or the couples themselves are too ashamed or embarrassed to bring up issues of such an intimate nature, and therefore many problems go unresolved.

In Judaism the burden of emotional and sexual satisfaction falls mainly on the husband, with the woman's satisfaction as priority. The marriage scene in the movie *Yentl* gives us a glimpse of this attitude. Just prior to the marriage, Barbra Streisand (who is posing as a man) is being instructed by her (his) male friend on the details of proper sexual etiquette, including how the man must be gentle, never forceful or selfish, taking his time in consideration of his wife's desires and readiness. Candidly speaking, it is considered the husband's obligation to satisfy his wife first, including experiencing an orgasm. It is for this reason that Judaism has traditionally been sympathetic and compassionate toward women who have undergone years of misery in sleeping with a man who is impotent, sexually brutal, or who forces her to do things that violate her conscience. In such cases separation or divorce has been granted, since, according to covenantal conditions, the husband has broken the terms of covenant. This may also include expecting her to have intercourse with him simply to relieve himself when she is emotionally neglected or abused. She is also justified to request divorce if he is personally unhygienic or has some type of repulsive habit that makes sex unbearable to her.

By the same token, neither the man nor the woman should use or withhold sex for manipulative purposes. If there is a season of abstinence it should be by mutual agreement or protocol (see 1 Corinthians 7: 3-6). This might involve menstruation, illness, or fasting. However, there are more cases than we know of in which couples who, because of physical or sexual difficulties or conditions, agree to live in a sexless marriage. The Bible makes it clear that this is not the ideal; in fact, it is not recommended since either partner may be all the more tempted to step outside the bounds of marriage out of sexual frustration. However, if both partners agree to the arrangement and can live in such a manner in peace and without resentment, there is no violation. In fact, the apostle Paul comments regarding advice along these lines, "I say this as a concession, not as a commandment." (1 Corinthians 7:6).

THE SIGN

Notwithstanding, the sexual act is a very important aspect in marriage because sex is a sign or symptom of the marital *condition*—it is not the marriage itself. What a misconception many couples have of this today, and especially men who do not see the woman's perspective! Men often consider sex to be the same as love, whereas women consider love to be affection and respect. As a result, a man may presume his marriage to be on safe ground as long as he is getting sex. He may not realize that just because his wife is allowing the act to go ahead, it does not mean that she is not bitterly unhappy and miserable.

Many times I have heard women cry, "He ignores (mocks, abuses, mistreats, etc.) me, but come bedtime, he expects me to have sex with him as if nothing is wrong. It makes me feel like I'm nothing but a prostitute." Judaism is so in tune to this sentiment that Jewish sages insisted that a man draw up a marriage contract or *ketubah* to ensure proper treatment of the wife, and that a marriage without such a guarantee "should be regarded as prostitution".[32] This does not imply that the wife is regarded as a prostitute but rather that she is being used like one.

This is tied in directly with the way a man approaches intimacy. It is essential, in order to have a truly healthy sexual relationship, that the woman is made to feel that she is uniquely special to her partner. For example, if a man is constantly looking at other women or commenting on them, the result is a chipping away of his wife's self esteem. Although she may be very attractive, this behavior will eventually destroy her confidence and security in the relationship. When this happens she will begin to push the man away, since, consciously or subconsciously, she is afraid that he will see what in her mind are imperfections that will turn him off. Therefore, a word of advice to men: if you want intimacy to be strong in your marriage, you must reaffirm your love and delight for your woman, and only her, and not only in the bedroom! A woman knows when she is genuinely loved, and very few women find that type of affection hard to resist.

To summarize, remember that signs and sacrifices were an important aspect of covenants since they were the physical symbols or representations that acted as a seal or witness to the agreement. The sign was often intertwined with a sacrificial element of the covenant as an indication of acceptance by the recipient (or "lesser") partner of that sacrifice. For example, the shedding of blood through circumcision is the sign of the covenant between God and Abraham (Genesis 17: 10, 11), as was the consummation of the sacrifice offered by Abraham to God (Genesis 15: 17, 18). Blood and consummation are often familiar signs of an offered and accepted sacrifice between partners in covenant.

It was no different in the marriage covenant. To this day, whether we are aware of it or not, we give the same consideration to those traditions. Even in our own laws, marriage is not valid until consummated, and some cultures still demand the evidence of spilled blood after consummation on the wedding night. In another perspective, the Bible says that the life is in the blood. This also directly ties in with sacrifice, since the man is to give his life for his wife—in other words, "give his blood." If this caring, sacrificial element dies or is lacking in a marriage and the wife therefore feels as though she is of little worth to him, one of the first signs is that the woman no longer wants sexual intimacy with her husband. Many husbands presume that the marriage is over when their wife is no longer sleeping with him; yet the reality is that she is no longer sleeping with him because the marriage has already died. In other words, it is a sign that the covenant has already been broken in some form.

THE SACRIFICE

In the covenantal relationship it is required that one partner (usually the "greater") provides a sacrifice while the recipient partner (the "lesser/weaker") either accepts or rejects it (obviously if the sacrifice is rejected, the covenant is not established). Therefore, it is both the offering *and* acceptance of the sacrifice that binds the covenant. But remember that a covenant was based on mutual agreement, not force, coercion, threat, or bullying. In other words, each partner was equally important to the covenant; only their roles were different.

This tells us that agreements in marriage should be arrived at mutually. The husband who bullies or beats his wife to get his way (in other words, violates her) is breaking covenant. This is strongly reflected in the book of Malachi where God confronts the abusive husband. Ironically, other verses from this section are selectively used to coerce women to stay in abusive marriages under the premise that if she seeks a divorce she is sinning. For that reason it is essential that we look at the entirety of the context. As we examine this passage you will see the covenantal setting that is otherwise overlooked, especially in Christian circles. The text is from Malachi 2:13–16 (CJB).

> *Here is something else you do: you cover ADONAI's[3] altar with tears, with weeping and with sighing, because he no longer looks at the offering or receives your gift with favor. Nevertheless you ask "Why is this?"*
>
> *Because ADONAI is witness between you and the wife of your youth that you have broken faith with her, though she is your companion, your wife by covenant. And hasn't he made [them] one [flesh] in order to have spiritual blood-relatives? For what the one [flesh] seeks is a seed from God. Therefore, take heed to your spirit, and don't break faith with the wife of your youth. "For I hate divorce," says ADONAI the God of Isra'el, "and him who covers his clothing with violence," says ADONAI-TZVA'OT (the Lord of Hosts). Therefore take heed to your spirit, and don't break faith.*

The context of this scripture is that God is neither listening to the prayers of a man nor blessing him for any sacrifices or offerings he brings, and therefore the man is distraught and weeping, wondering why. In response, God tells him that it is because he has broken faith with his wife, his covenant partner, and therefore no longer qualifies, if you will,

---

[3] Adonai is the holy name of God, translated in English as LORD.

to receive the blessings. Remember that in our original definition of covenant at the beginning of this section, it was stated that covenants are accompanied by blessings for obedience and curses for disobedience. From these verses it is obvious that part of the blessings in the marriage covenant is for God to answer the prayers and accept the offerings of the husband on behalf of himself and his family. If, however, a husband is disobedient or breaks the covenant with his wife, the opposite happens.

Peter refers directly to this in one of his letters to the believers in early Christianity: "Likewise you husbands, dwell with them [*your wives*] with understanding, giving honor to the wife, as to *the weaker vessel* [the "lesser" role as recipient], and as being *heirs together* [equal covenant partners] of the grace of life, *that your prayers may not be hindered*" (1 Peter 3:7, brackets and italics mine for emphasis). Why was Peter taking the time and effort to explain this to those to whom he was writing his letter? For the same reason, Paul goes into detail in many of his letters to the Greek, Roman and other Gentile converts: because they were unfamiliar with Judaic teaching and precept, including the Scriptures and covenantal arrangements! Remember once again that early Christianity was a Jewish sect; therefore, once you begin interpreting their instructions in that context, they suddenly make more sense.

Let us continue the analysis of the Malachi verses.

The final verses end up with another statement by God: He hates divorce. This is the verse that churches use to justify their teaching that divorce is a sin and therefore always wrong. However, let us look at the complete statement. God begins by saying that He hates divorce but immediately completes the sentence with the statement that He also hates when a man "covers his clothing with violence." One of the basic provisions listed in Scripture that a husband is obligated to give his wife is clothing. By association of reference then, "clothing" here is implied to also mean the man's wife, which is how it is actually translated in some Bibles. Also recall what implications were behind that provision—that a husband was not to shame or humiliate his wife but rather protect and esteem her. We can safely presume, then, that the husband whom the Lord is addressing in this statement is mistreating his wife and not rendering the honor due her. Moreover, he is denying or trying to hide the fact. The word "covers" in this Scripture has the basic meaning of covering up, hiding or concealing something, and the word for violence (*chamas*) refers not only to oppression or cruelty but also injustice or lack of fair treatment in general.[33]

A final clarification of the word "hate" is also needed before we transpose that verse into our own modern dialect. The word "hate" here is the same used in verses such as "Jacob I have loved but Esau I have hated" and Jesus' statement in Luke that unless "one hates his father or mother he cannot be my disciple" (the Greek word for hate used in the Gospel is the equivalent of the Hebrew). Although the word does mean a strong dislike or disfavor, it is also used to signify preference—and that usually based on value or character. In other words, the "hated" thing has or should have less value in relation to what it is compared to. Jesus clarifies this concept found in the passage from Luke cited above with a similar statement in Matthew: "He who loves father or mother more than Me is not worthy of Me" (10:37).

Therefore, according to the verses in Malachi, although divorce is deplorable to God because of the pain and disruption it causes, a man's mistreatment of a woman is just as or even more disgusting to God, especially if he denies it or tries to cover up the truth. The man who does so has violated covenant and therefore forfeits any blessings from God or the community. In fact, we will see in our section on divorce that, within both Judaism and early Christianity, a man was compelled to release his wife if he was found to be abusive or negligent. As the Malachi verse states, divorce may not be the preference, but it certainly is better than chaining another human being to a life of hell.

We have seen so far that it is the man, as the greater covenant partner, who is expected to provide or offer sacrifice in the marriage. The woman's role, as the so-called "weaker" or "lesser" vessel, is to accept the sacrifice in order to make the covenant binding. This aspect of covenant has not only been sorely misrepresented, it has been totally set upside down, especially in Christian teaching. In most marriages it is usually the woman who makes most of the sacrifices. Did you know that statistically, women and children represent those in greatest poverty and malnourishment worldwide? Did you know that this is largely due to the fact that when there is food in the house men eat first, then children (because the mother forfeits her portion for them), and the woman eats whatever is left, if anything? Did you know that, between genders, women and little girls are the least cared for and educated while men and boys have precedence? Why? Because it is presumed that their value is inferior to that of males.

Unfortunately, this attitude has been reinforced by the way the church has presented marriage, with the woman rather than the man making the most sacrifices. Again, this comes from the way scriptures, especially from the New Testament, are interpreted and used by the church to urge wives to submit to their husbands regardless of circumstances, even in the face of poverty, neglect, maltreatment or violence.

Let us take a look at another scripture commonly used to justify this position:

> *Wives, submit to your own husbands, as to the Lord. For the husband is head of the wife, as also Christ is head of the church; and He is Savior of the body. Therefore, just as the church is subject to Christ, so let the wives be to their own husbands in everything."* (Ephesians 5:22–24))

In this passage the relationship between husband and wife is compared to the relationship between Christ (Messiah) and his believers. However, when these verses are presented, most of the time what is not mentioned is that the Lord is faithful and therefore believers can fully trust him since he only ever has their best interests at heart. In fact, one of the titles of Christ is Shepherd. Just as sheep trust the shepherd to guard and protect them, even to the point of sacrificing himself for their safety, so should a woman be able to completely trust in her husband's covenantal role as provider and protector. If she can fully trust him with her well-being, then she knows she can also trust his opinion on the various issues of life. (It should also be noted here that the words "to their own husbands" refers to the fact that a woman has covenantal obligation only between herself and her husband and is therefore not subject to any man in general.) Again, these instructions to the wife are often quoted to women, yet the verses immediately following concerning the greater role of the man are rarely ever cited:

> Husbands, love your wives, *just as Christ also loved the church* and gave Himself for her, *that He might sanctify* (set it apart as special) *and cleanse her with the washing of water by the word, that He might present her to Himself a glorious church, not having spot or wrinkle or any such thing, but that she should be holy and without blemish.* So husbands ought to love their own wives as their own bodies; *he who loves his wife loves himself. For no one ever hated his own flesh, but* nourishes (remember the meaning!) *and cherishes it, just as the Lord does the church. For we are members of His body, of His flesh and of His bones.*[4] *For this reason a man shall leave his father and mother and be joined to his wife, and the two shall become one flesh....Nevertheless let each one of you in particular* **so love his own wife as himself,** *and let the wife see that* she respects *her husband.* (Ephesians 5:25–31, 33, emphasis and brackets mine)

With the background of knowledge we now have of Judaic covenant, it is easy to see that the above passage is describing the covenant roles each is expected to fulfill in the marriage. The husband, as the "greater" partner in that covenant, has the greater level of responsibility and sacrifice. In fact, these scriptures state that the man is to love his wife to the point of self-sacrifice, forfeiting his own personal comfort, putting her needs before his own. It is very difficult not to respect a man who does this, and a woman knows that she can safely give deference to the love of such a man. It is in this sense that she places herself "under" him, much in the way someone is under a protective covering such as a tent or shelter.

This deference is often translated as "submission," yet the way the church has interpreted and presented these verses has turned submission into a dirty word. This includes the already-mentioned beliefs and

---

[4] We will be looking at the importance of the phraseology of being one's own "flesh and bone" and "becoming one flesh" further down.

expectations that women should make all or most of the sacrifices in a marriage, and that only men have final authority in decision-making. Such ideas have turned the covenantal meaning of submission into subjection or slavery. Let us remember that there are also scriptures that state that *both* wives and husbands (as well as male and female believers in the New Testament) should submit *equally* to each other (Ephesians 5:21), but these are rarely mentioned.

Our society has confused personal value with job or work value rather than regarding roles as mere assignments of duty. Hence, the term "weaker" vessel came to mean someone who *is* weak. In terms of marriage, this means the woman. But does Scripture really call women "weak"? In Genesis 2:18 we find the role of the woman in terms of her relationship to her male partner described as "a helper comparable to him." The Hebrew word usually translated here as 'helper' is *ezer*. However, various sources, including Friedman and others, point out that the word also means "strength."[34] For example, the same word is translated synonymously in reference to God as one's "helper" or one's "strength." A good English equivalent, then, would be "support," since a support not only helps but must also be strong in order to do its job.

Think about it. If the support one leans on is weaker than the one leaning on it, it will break; therefore, a support must be stronger than the person or thing leaning on it. This affirms the rabbinical explanation for why the Bible tells the man to cleave to his wife and not the wife to her husband. In fact, Hayter mentions how some feminists have even used this very argument to prove that women are superior to men! The phrase usually translated as "a helper suitable or comparable to him" is translated by Jewish sources as "a strength corresponding to him," with the word "corresponding" meaning equal and not inferior to. Therefore, a man's wife is someone who is his equal (as a person) yet who has the strength to support him. In fact, many Jewish writings consider women to be stronger in terms of emotional and intuitive ability.

The second chapter of Genesis ends with the man declaring the woman to be bone of his bones and flesh of his flesh, closing with the biblical decree that, because of this, a man leaves his father and his mother and clings to his wife, resulting in them becoming one flesh. This is often interpreted as simply the description of how Eve was physically drawn out and formed from Adam's body. Many people also assume that the reference to one flesh implies sexual union. This is an incomplete translation, for it is much more profound. While it is true that the phrase "becoming one" can refer to sexual union, sexual intercourse alone does not imply covenant. In fact because of this, many people question whether commitment or marriage between a man and woman in intimate relationship is even important, pointing out that Adam and Eve were never "married." Or were they? In ancient times when partners entered into covenant they considered the other person to be as their own body (flesh and bone) and of the same mind. That is why the verses we just read from Paul's letter to the Ephesians specify that a man must love his wife *as his own body*. In other words, it was as if the two were "one" and the same person. This terminology and practice is affirmed throughout the Bible. For example, when the elders of Israel wanted to make a covenant with David, they approached him with the phrase, "Indeed we are your bone and your flesh" (1 Chronicles 11:1–3). Adam's remark that Eve was bone of his bone and flesh of his flesh, as well as the fact that the two are described as becoming one flesh, are declarative evidence that their relationship was one of covenant—a "marriage," if you will.

So far we have seen that, according to covenant standards, the wife has a recipient or responsive role. In other words, her role is reflective as opposed to instigative in function. Interestingly, women are symbolized in the Bible by the moon (Gen. 37: 9–10) which itself has reflective qualities and beauty. That is why in Judaism, especially throughout Scripture, a wife is often referred to as the glory of her husband, the word glory implying a reflective quality. Therefore, if a man is a good husband, it will be reflected in the countenance of his wife. Show me a happy wife and more than likely she will have a loving companion for a husband. Show me a wife who appears bedraggled and depressed, bitter or sad, and more than likely you will find that she is unloved (Proverbs 30:23).

As mentioned earlier, women have traditionally had less command-ments or obligations imposed upon them in Judaism. Even in the early

New Testament writings the demands are few and direct: respect and love your husband. As we have discovered, this respect is in response to the sacrificial love the husband gives his wife, and that love is then reciprocated from the recipient partner as a sign of their acceptance of that sacrifice. For the wife, this means not taking for granted the good things a caring and respectable husband gives, including all types of provision. The woman who squanders what her husband has worked hard for is violating the trust of the marriage covenant; yet, I have seen households where the man, upon returning home from work, enters a messy home with no food prepared and is also expected to bathe the kids and put them to bed, all while the woman is at home. In our quest to liberate women from the confines of the home we must be careful not to throw the baby out with the bathwater, so to speak, and abuse or neglect the contributions made by a faithful husband.

I am also fully aware, however, of the double day many women put in working at a job and then coming home and doing most or all of the housework. That is also an imbalance. If it is necessary for a woman to bring in extra income, other duties should be shared. As for looking after the children, both parents must have equal input. This is not only so that a woman is not overburdened, it is healthy and beneficial for children to have a solid relationship with their father, and developing a relationship means spending time and doing things together.

So what about the age-old debate about whether or not a wife should go out and work? The traditional view among many fundamental religious groups is that a woman's place is in the home. I personally know women whose husbands have either forbidden them to be employed or who despise it although they do not stop it. Yet the barefoot and pregnant woman in the kitchen is not the prototype "wife of noble character" portrayed in Proverbs 31, who not only ran her own business but also kept her profits to use as she saw fit. In fact, Judaism teaches that a woman must contribute in some way to the household. This not only benefits the couple economically but also prevents the husband from being overburdened and encourages the couple to set goals and work toward them together. There are no hard and fast rules stating exactly how a woman ought to help; these issues must be discussed and solutions arrived at mutually by the couple themselves. For example, many traditional women do not have paid employment outside the home, yet they contribute in other ways such as cooking meals from scratch or doing other things with their hands. The key here is mutual respect and cooperation that benefits the entire family.

As intense as this chapter has been, it really has only scratched the surface, touching mainly on the history of marriage and pertinent roles of women in Christianity which have sprung from the roots of Judaism. We also saw how those Judaic roots have often been wrongfully applied or interpreted due to the lack of understanding of covenantal structure and the abandonment of Judaic elements within Christianity. This may have given some of you answers as to why your husband or society has confined you as a woman to an inferior role in your marriage, but there is another important aspect of this that needs to be discussed. It is the fact that women themselves have become so accustomed to tolerating these injustices that they contribute to keeping themselves chained through the thoughts and attitudes of their own hearts.

Ironically, many chained women often view their motives and ideas to be correct, even noble. Living with all good intention and always trying to do the right thing, they wonder why they are not getting positive results. Their husbands are no more affectionate or understanding toward them, and even their pleas to God to intervene in their marriage seem to go unheeded. If they are the obedient and submissive wives they are supposed to be, why are they not being rewarded? If you are a woman of faith who has ever struggled with these thoughts, then the next section may be the most important one you will ever read.

POWERS
WITHIN THE
UNIVERSE

Part Three

In the previous section we saw how covenant roles of marriage are determined according to Scripture. We have also seen how these elements have been wrongly interpreted and applied to church doctrine over the centuries by converts who were not raised with knowledge of Judaic culture. As a result, many faith communities (and society in general) have developed and adopted the perspective that wives play an inferior role in marriage and are therefore obligated to submit to their husbands even in situations of neglect or abuse. Scriptures that have been taken out of context are often used to justify this position. This leaves the woman of faith in a predicament: either she continues to submit to the authority of her faith and her husband, or she leaves the marriage and is usually ostracized as a result. If she does stay, it is likely that she will face a life sentence of unspeakable stress and demeaning treatment.

Mother Theresa said it well when she stated that rejection is one of the most difficult things that a human being can be subjected to. Given that, we have a world full of married women who live with rejection every single day of their lives because they are unloved. To add insult to injury, not only are they denied due respect from their husbands—the very ones they look to for affection and love—they are often further rejected by their faith community and even friends and family if they complain and want to leave.

The most difficult blow, however, is when many of these women are also rejected by their own children. Why? One would presume that children would have sympathy for a mistreated mother. Tragically, it appears to be a human characteristic to despise what is perceived as weakness, and as a result, the mother who is degraded by her husband often gains little or no respect in the eyes of her children. If anything, children may actually hate and blame the mother for staying in a marriage of misery, a situation in which they are also forced to live. Ironically, staying for the sake of the children is one of the reasons women give for remaining in a bad marriage.

Women who do remain in conditions of maltreatment, and who cause their children to undergo the same, often do so out of genuine motives. In other words, they really think they are doing the right thing. This is especially so with women of faith. If you would ask women who have endured either abuse or emotional neglect in their personal relationships why they chose to stay rather than leave, you would find that most, if not all, have had some noble reason. Contrary to popular reactions—"She just wants to be a martyr" or "she must like it because she stays"—these women do *not* like what they are going through. Instead, they have convinced themselves that not only is it reasonable to stay, it is necessary. Although most of their reasons are tied in with elements of faith, it is not always so. Many non-religious women also use some of the same justifications, although they seem to be more strongly reinforced in the minds of devout women because of certain faith teachings.

Let me note before we move along that, although I at times refer to leaving an unstable situation, I believe that the first option should be for the couple to seek counseling and attempt to repair the marriage.

However, there are situations in which only one or neither partner wants to work toward change. It is often at this point that those who are trying to help the couple get frustrated. If separation is forbidden or never considered as a way out, the incentive for change is greatly limited.

Consider the scenario of a woman seeking help from those in authority at her faith community regarding some grievous situation in her marriage. Usually they initially sympathize with her and agree to speak to the husband. Obviously, if the husband heeds their advice or rebuke, the matter is worked through and resolved and the equilibrium of the marriage is restored. Unfortunately, if the husband has a very controlling or selfish nature, he will balk at their advice, at times even reacting against the involved authorities and intimidating them. Others manipulate the "system" by pretending to make a turn-around. They begin to put forward a positive image to the involved faith community, at times even attending religious services and events, all the while remaining the same type of person in the home.

In these latter two circumstances, if the woman persists in returning with the complaint that the situation has not improved (or has worsened because the husband's anger has been raised) it is at this point that a fundamental shift occurs in the situation, usually to the detriment of the woman. The faith elders or advisors become frustrated with the situation because they can no longer see any solution and are therefore left with a feeling of helplessness. Since they cannot seem to make the husband comply and because leaving one's spouse is not considered an option, the common response is to throw the problem back into the lap of the woman. I personally know of more than one woman who has been told at this point by her minister or faith advisor, "Just submit to your husband and do what you're told!" What they do not consider is that the threat of actually losing his spouse may be the only thing that motivates a neglectful or abusive husband to change. Not only do people of faith need to acknowledge this as a viable option, it should be considered a necessary action when the safety and well-being of the wife and others in the family are threatened.

On the other hand, it is not always only the husband that refuses to let his wife go. As mentioned earlier, it is often a woman's own decision to remain in a bad marriage. Some of the most common reasons include staying for the children, having a sense of duty or love for one's husband, fear of committing a grave sin by leaving, or simply because the very thought of leaving raises up emotions of sheer terror.

Motivating factors from within the woman's own emotions and thinking can also play an important role in keeping her chained. These include a low self-image, an incorrect perception of love, even an element of pride. Although this may be difficult to face, these issues need to be addressed by the woman or she will remain shackled to them forever. Regardless of whether or not she remains in her current miserable marriage or chooses to leave, she will take those same thought patterns and attitudes along with her and will continue to repeat the behaviors, ending up with the same miserable results over and over again. This also applies even when her husband does decide to change. He will find her responding to him in the only way she knows how—as a victim.

I realize this is difficult for some of you to read because you have endured years of suffering or neglect and you feel the last thing you need is to have someone point a finger at you. Do not look at these statements as accusations but rather descriptions of what you have unwittingly been formed to become. You have the sympathy and understanding of people who know that you have adopted those thought patterns and reactions as a means of survival; however you cannot stay in fighting mode forever. God desires that we live in peace, and freeing ourselves from within is the first step to finding that peace. With that, I believe it is essential that we examine the motives of the heart that persuade women that they are doing the right thing in staying, and more importantly, tolerating the damaging behavior in their relationships.

There are certain fundamental principles that exist in the universe which apply to life regardless of whether or not you adhere to a religious faith. One of those principles is the force or law of love. Have you ever wondered why the most well-meaning and sacrificial people are often the ones who are stepped on or mistreated? The underlying reason for this has to do not so much with love itself but with what we perceive to be love. Most people think of love as an emotion or action with good intention; therefore, if they have strong feelings toward someone or something and do favors for them, they expect to get approval or love in return. They quickly get frustrated, angry or hurt if their efforts fail. However, love is neither simply emotion nor intention but rather a universal law or principle. In order to get positive results, then, we must act according to the rules of that principle.

Take flying as an example. Simply wanting or believing hard enough that you can fly, or imitating birds by jumping off a cliff and flapping your arms, will not give you that ability; rather, discovering and putting into practice the laws of aerodynamics will make flight possible. In other words, good intention or faith alone, even if accompanied by much work or effort, does not necessarily make the right thing happen. There are many women out there who have sacrificed and slaved at pleasing their husband and being the "perfect" wife and mother, all with negative results. If you are one of them, perhaps it is time you considered the possibility that what you thought was love is actually something else.

The Bible says that God is Love. If He is the personification of love, then we need to look at His character to discover what love really is. First of all, God does not force Himself on people; we have free will. This means that He doesn't jump down from Heaven and interrupt people when they are doing wrong. Unfortunately, this is the very reason why He is blamed when bad things happen. A prime characteristic of love, then, is that it operates in and through free will or choice. Love, therefore, cannot be forced or coerced upon someone.

In other words, you cannot "make" someone love you. The man who persists in stalking and harassing a woman or who thinks that dozens of roses will somehow magically make her want him is deceiving himself. So is the woman who thinks that she will be loved or appreciated by her husband and family if only she does more or does better. It is very common for a mistreated, emotionally wounded or neglected woman to have the outwardly perfect home, often spotless and over-organized. She herself can also appear to be an over-achiever or dress meticulously. Now, do not go around assuming that every woman who is a good dresser or who keeps a well-run home is abused or neglected! Rather, I am saying that a woman who is desperately seeking love and approval often gives off a perfect image in order to gain that approval. This may even stem from wounds inflicted upon her heart previous to the marriage. This is especially characteristic among women who belong to a faith community where there is constant reinforcement of what the ideal family home should be like.

Listen carefully: If your husband or someone else does not love you, it is not necessarily because of anything you are doing or failing to do. Trying to make yourself fit in their mold or become more acceptable in their eyes does not guarantee that they will respond in the way you want anyway, so stop degrading yourself.

Another aspect of God is that He is just—another word for being fair. This is where we get the word "justice" from. This aspect of love is often one of the most misunderstood, which causes many people to end up in messy relationships. Being just or fair means responding rightly to each situation. When we think of justice, we think of how unfair it would be for someone who has caused grievous loss or injury or who mistreats others to get away with it. We are also especially angered at the thought of an innocent person being punished or hurt when they do not deserve it. God thinks the same way. Proverbs 17:15 says, "He who justifies the wicked, and he who condemns the just, both of them alike are an abomination to the Lord."

Although most of us would say we agree with this scripture, scores of people violate it almost every day by tolerating and even covering up for someone else's abusive and irresponsible behavior. I know many women who are shocked when they realize that what they thought to be love or obedience was actually covering up for evil. It is easy for women to be deceived this way since many faith organizations teach that it is the duty of a faithful and loving wife to serve her husband without question and to overlook his flaws. Sadly, that attitude has also permeated society in general. I remember a woman telling me that, regardless of whether or not your husband is right, it is the duty of the wife to stand by him. Not only was her husband physically and verbally abusive toward her, few people could stand his presence because of his overbearing and insolent character. To this day I cannot stand the song "Stand By Your Man," a song that aptly describes this attitude and the lives of many women who believe this. The stunning lesson women need to draw out from this principle is that, contrary to what you were led to believe, *you are not pleasing God* in that form of submission. If letting the guilty off the hook is as repulsive to God as blaming an innocent person, then naturally you will not be rewarded for protecting or defending your husband's bad behavior, even if you have good intentions.

A woman once told me how her little girl asked constantly why God did not answer their prayers for her daddy to change. Not only did that woman not understand that God will not force someone to change because we all have free will, as long as you cover up for evil, even in your husband, God can no more answer your prayers than He can the prayers of the covenant-breaking husband mentioned in the previous section. To ask Him to do so would be to expect Him to go against His very nature.

Some of you may think our dedication to someone requires us to show love unconditionally and sacrificially—especially to a spouse, even when they do wrong. After all, is not God also a God of mercy? Sacrificial love is indeed noble and admirable, *but it is only considered as such when it is done for a just or righteous cause, never for an evil one.* In other words, its glory comes *because* it is resisting evil, not covering up for it! Therefore, you can be the most selfless and sacrificial person around, but if your motives and actions are not being carried out through the principle of love, that is, according to justice and the truth, they are futile and even destructive. God is fully aware that we are imperfect and often misguided, and that is where His mercy comes in. Mercy reveals why people do certain things; however, it never goes so far as to condone or make excuses for offensive and bad behavior. In other words, mercy says I understand why you have done what you have done but it never says it is all right to keep doing it if it is harmful. So, if we are not acting in love when we do those things, what are we doing, then?

There is another principle at work in the universe. It is the power of fear, love's complete opposite. Whereas love is positive and deals in truth and honesty, fear is negative and thrives in denial, deception and lying. Whereas love sets you on a path of stability and confidence, a life governed by fear will be one of insecurity and uncertainty. Although we have the free will to choose either love or fear, once we submit to the power of fear it has the unique ability to paralyze us against action.

Fear is the basis for most, if not all, of the reasons for staying in an oppressive or unhappy relationship. That is why it is essential for the chained woman to face and overcome her fears. Often, however, she cannot do it alone. A woman contemplating leaving needs a good support system of friends and groups that will help her stabilize the various areas in her life. Let us look again at the reasons for staying, this time drawing out the motives of fear behind them.

Most people presume that couples who stay together supposedly for the children do so primarily because they believe it's in the family's best interest not to split the home. While this may be true in some cases, more often than not there are stronger, underlying reasons that even the man or woman may not immediately recognize in themselves. These reasons are actually deep-seated fears of the hurdles they know they will have to face if one of them leaves. To the woman it is the fear of being unable to support and care for her children as head of her own household, and to the man it is the dread of being alone.

Children are a major barrier to the woman who wants to leave. Since it is the mother who usually ends up being the primary caregiver, this means that she will end up carrying the financial and emotional burden of raising the children, including the constant dilemma of finding and affording suitable and timely child-care. This is especially difficult for the woman who has not developed or maintained employment skills throughout her marriage for whatever reason. The idea of going out and getting a job is daunting to her, especially when she discovers that she will have to work two, if not three, low-paying jobs in order to make ends meet.

Even women who have maintained full-time employment find it difficult. Statistically, women earn only about seventy percent of the wages a man does for the same type of work. That is why female-headed homes rank the highest in poverty levels. The rare exception is when a woman receives sufficient spousal and child support payments from her former partner. This is rare because it requires two things from the man that often do not simultaneously exist: a sufficient income and a willingness to pay. Another major stumbling block often not considered is the fact that the majority of women, even those with higher education or established employment, remain surprisingly ignorant when it comes to handling their own personal finances.

Aside from the financial hurdles, most women who leave discover that they struggle with maintaining control of the children. Often, by the time a marriage breaks down to the point where either the woman or the man finally leaves the family home, the children have little or no respect for her. As a result, many mothers face an extra burden of rebelling, disruptive children who seem to deliberately work against her. Ironically, therefore, many women decide that it is actually easier for them to stay and endure the neglect or abuse of the marital relationship and suffer the knowledge of their children's rejection than to be confronted with even more stress and failure in their life. This is at times magnified by a further underlying feeling of guilt that she will be taking the children away from their father, especially if she recognizes their resentment toward her. Since most mothers, especially insecure ones, seek ways to win their children's approval and love, they actually come to believe that they are making a genuine sacrifice for their children by remaining in a personally unhappy marriage.

Regarding the male perspective, I have been told by men that one of their greatest fears is being left alone, especially once they have become accustomed to always having someone around. This is more so in the case of the emotionally insecure man. As a result, and depending upon the individual's personality, he will either beg his wife to stay or manipulate her into doing so, even to the point of threatening her. Staying for the children, therefore, can actually be a conscious or subconscious cover-up for the parents' own fears, including the fear of appearing like a failure.

As I was growing up I heard stories of how some of my parents' contemporaries were dreadfully unhappy in their marriages, yet "stayed for the children." I heard others judging these people and was guilty of joining them in their perspective. Now that I am a mature adult and have seen and experienced many things, I have come to understand that there is so much more beneath the surface and have stopped judging them.

The second reason why women stay in unhappy or abusive relationships is that they are genuinely convinced that it is their duty to stand by their man. Staying and tolerating his behavior is their way of proving their love and devotion to him. We have seen in the first part of this section that this stems from the false notion that if you love someone you will do *anything* for them. Women of faith are perfect targets for this since traditional teachings on submission not only reinforce that idea but also falsely claim that God will reward the woman simply for submitting even if her husband is asking her to accept or do something that violates her in any way.

Some years ago a book written by a minister's wife on that very topic circulated among some women in our neighborhood. Many began to do everything and anything their husbands wanted based on the isolated verse we referenced earlier: "Wives, submit to your husbands in everything." Naturally, as in many cases, the rest of that scripture, which outlines the man's responsibility to love his wife as his own body, was not mentioned. Instead, the duty of submission was based solely on gender. The results of unquestioningly obeying this teaching ranged from mere failure to disaster. Abusive husbands viewed this newly found submission as proof and justification of their unquestionable right to dominate their wives and treat them any way they wanted simply on the basis that they were men. Women who had depended on religious services or other support groups for moral and emotional support and whose husbands did not like it but had previously not prevented them from going, suddenly stopped attending because they now viewed it as an act of disobedience or disrespect to their husbands. They reasoned that it must have been this previous "disobedience" on their part as to why God had not rewarded them and changed their husbands.

One of the most surprising and unexpected results was how manipulative some of these women became. One shared how she learned to get things from her husband by begging or whining, under the guise of being as submissive as a child. Others made their husbands their favorite dishes and catered to them before asking for money or telling them about something they had bought. Eventually most of the households returned to their original conditions, with some exceptions. Sadly, some of the women lost what little respect or power they had to begin with, and their lives and relationships with their husbands actually worsened.

What these women did not realize is that their behavior was not based on the universal principle of love and was therefore doomed to fail. Firstly, they presumed that God would somehow override their husbands' right to free will and "make" them see the light as some kind of reward for their obedience. Everyone has free will. No amount of prayers or faith will force someone to change.

Now don't get me wrong, I am a fervent believer in the power of prayer but I also believe that it can and will only work within the principles and powers set down in the universe by our Almighty God. Sometimes it is very clear that there has been some sort of spiritual intervention in the lives of some people—this is answered prayer. However, how each individual responds is totally his or her own choice. Not even God can make someone do something they are unwilling to do.

Remember also the other aspect of God's love—justice, which involves truth. Most of these women, regardless of whether or not their intentions were good, were manipulating, not loving. There is a difference. Manipulation is a fruit of fear because it acts through deception, sneakiness and lying. It tries to get the other person to do something they normally would not do if they were not pressured. When an individual has little or no power and they cannot get what they want from someone or they want to avoid the truth, they will manipulate. This is a common characteristic in homes where there is an imbalance of power among members or where there is an abuser or abusers who are never challenged or confronted for their actions.

Just remember that the motive behind love is to do what is right and to benefit everyone involved. This includes confronting a negligent or abusive person, especially if they are a family member. To leave such an individual to themselves is to allow them to become the type of person others despise. Why would we ever want that for those we love? This is an aspect of love that many of us either fail to recognize or want to avoid. Genuine love often does not appear to be our idea of love. Since love deals in truth, speaking it will, at times, open up the proverbial can of worms. It confronts injustice, unfairness and wrong-doing that damages us or others or that promotes unhealthy behavior. As a result, an act of genuine love will often create division between individuals.

Let me illustrate with a story. A woman who was terminally ill was visited by a neighbor who attempted to talk to her about some personal issues she felt this woman needed to address before she passed on. The woman was very affronted by this. Knowing who her neighbor was, I asked the woman whether or not she thought the intentions of this person were genuine. "Does she care for you?" I asked.

Without hesitation the answer was "Yes."

"Then do you think she also knew that talking to you might make you angry and even cost your friendship?"

After thinking for only a minute, again the answer was, "Yes."

"Then this woman must really love you, because she wanted you to have peace even if it meant she might be hated or rejected for it."

The ill woman's face changed. "You know, I never looked at it that way before," she said.

No, we often do not look at it that way. Ironically, the one who loves you most is not always the sweet-talking and flattering individual, or even the person who never says anything even when things need to be said, but rather the individual who will speak the truth even if it means suffering for it. The results of this type of confrontation have far more effect than simply giving in.

If you are in an unhappy or unfair situation, simply praying about it but doing nothing to change it will lead nowhere. God wants us to stand up for what is right. In doing so we allow the flow of His power to come through; but when we protect wrong doing, it stops His power. When you stand up for what is right and begin to demand accountability for wrong behavior, you will notice that certain things will begin to happen that uncannily correspond to your prayers. Now, this still does not guarantee that the other person will respond correctly; however, even in that case, a fundamental change has occurred. Not only is the wrongdoer no longer able to manipulate, the responsibility and accountability of his or her actions are put back on him or her.

One woman shared how her husband would berate and threaten to leave her whenever she would bring up issues that were creating stress in their marriage. This was his way of avoiding the subject and stopping the discussion. Her normal reaction to his threats had always been to cry and beg him not to leave, a reaction based on fear. After discovering this principle, she began calling him on his threats. The next time he threatened to leave, she did not cry or beg but rather looked straight at him and said, "Fine, if you think it is that bad here, you can leave. Do you want me to get the suitcases out for you?" He fell silent and to this day has never threatened her with that again.

Your key to freedom is not in giving in to fear and its fruit—which includes manipulation and misplaced pity—it is in standing up for what is right. When your controller sees that he can no longer get to you and intimidate you, his power is broken. This may take a while. Individuals who are used to controlling or manipulating others to get their way do not readily give up that power. In fact, things may initially get worse before they get better because the struggle for power is heightened. Eventually, however, if they see their tactics are ineffective, they will back down.

A word of caution is important to address here. If you are dealing with a violent or potentially violent individual, you need to be more careful in your approach. This type of individual may react with force or physical violence, even murder, if they see they are cornered and their power is gone. In this case, my advice is to plan to leave quietly, without telling him your intentions. This is discussed below under the topic of staying because of fear. I do not mean to alarm you, but you need to be aware of the very real possibility of a potentially fatal outcome. Most women who are murdered are killed by their husband or partner, often immediately after they leave or threaten to leave. If you have the slightest inner feeling that he will harm you, listen to your instinct even if others feel you are exaggerating. It is better to be alive and wrong than dead and right.

The other strong link in the chain that keeps women bound is the belief that she is sinning if she leaves her marriage, even temporarily. She has been taught by her church or other faith authority that divorce is evil and an unredeemable sin. I have heard more than one woman lament the fact that she did not leave sooner because, "I was sure God was going to strike me down the minute I walked out the door." This is the mindset of fear and condemnation. The majority of women in a situation like this have been told that they are the reason the marriage is not working. Either they are not submissive enough or there is some other thing they must be doing wrong. Yet in these cases there is little or no enforced accountability upon the husband for his actions. This teaching especially exists in religions where the man's headship of the home is stressed and is never to be challenged or questioned. Remember our discussion of the covenantal structure of marriage: women are meant to be equal partners with the man.

Although divorce is discouraged in Scripture, it is never called a sin. Many people are surprised to see that, rather than divorce itself being condemned, it is the misuse and abuse of the process that men used in order to justify putting their wives away that was rebuked. God gave us the ideal pattern for the marital relationship in Genesis in which the covenant is described as the man and woman "becoming one." However, He knew that the ideal does not always happen and therefore divorce was given as a way out of a marital situation *that would otherwise cause us to sin.* This is described in Jesus' response to his disciples' question on marriage and divorce. First, Jesus cites the Genesis passage we just mentioned. Upon hearing this, his disciples asked why Moses then instructed them to write a bill of divorcement (Matthew 19:7). Jesus' reply was "because your hearts are hard." In other words, not all men would keep the ideal laid down in Scripture because of stubbornness and selfish motives and a hard heart. The sending away of a wife was originally intended for *her* sake, not the man's!

Although divorce is not God's preference, we will see that it is better than forcing another person to remain locked in a life of misery and oppression. In fact, if divorce is a sin, then God himself would be guilty. Jeremiah 3:8 describes how God wrote ancient Israel a certificate of divorce or putting away. Some of you may argue that these were merely symbolic words, but remember that a covenant is a covenant is a covenant, and if divorce was meant to be such a stigma, certainly God would not have used that analogy.[35] Moreover, in the book of Ezra, God *commands* His people to put away spouses who have led them away from following Him. It would seem, then, that these two biblical examples illustrate that God is more concerned with our moral conscience and our walk with Him than our marital status.

This reminds me of the story of a woman who was rebuked by an older male family member when she left her abusive marriage and filed for divorce. Although this man beat and abused his wife over the years and taught his children to steal and swindle, he was certain that, although she was in danger of eternal damnation, he was going to paradise after death because he had never divorced.

The final reason listed for not leaving is the terror of what type of repercussions it will bring. Sometimes women are afraid to leave simply because of insecurity; however, there are times when a woman has a legitimate concern that her husband will retaliate by hurting or even killing her.

If you are a woman in such a situation, you need to get out of the home. Staying with him will not stop him from killing you. While it is true that some women are killed when they do leave, there are just as many that are murdered by their partner while still living with him. In such a case, however, you need to use more strategy in leaving as previously mentioned. The first rule is not to tell your abuser that you are planning to leave, and especially do not tell him when. You also must have many things in place before you leave, such as a safe place to stay and a strong support network about you. If your partner is especially violent, you must never, ever consider going back, regardless of how much he pleads with you or appears to be remorseful.

Let this sink in. If he really did care about you, he would never have continued hurting you the way he has for years. And yes, he can help it. In this day and age there are more than enough groups and professionals that he can go to for counseling and personal help in areas such as anger management. You also need to realize as well that, even though he apologizes for abusing you *but never actually does anything about changing*, he is not convinced he is doing anything wrong, nor does he want to change. The pleading and the tears are only ploys to get you to feel sorry for him all over again. The lesson here is not to confuse love with pity, which is what many women do. Pity is feeling sorry for someone and is based on emotions; love is acting according to the truth regardless of our feelings.

Although we have uncovered some of the reasons women remain in unwholesome or even dangerous marriages, these are not necessarily the only reasons or motives they may have. My main objective was to point out the differences between the forces of love and fear and how they influence our thinking and even our actions. With this knowledge you can now test your heart and mind to see whether you are thinking and acting in ways that benefit you and your family or allowing the destructive power of fear and manipulation to continue ruining your life. As you recognize yourself in these situations, especially those that are more serious or potentially dangerous, I suggest that you immediately seek advice and support from friends or family members that you can trust. Find assistance from groups that specialize in dealing with these issues. They will have materials that will go deeper into detail and further help you escape.

Confronting and testing the way we think was also meant as an exercise to prepare you for the next section, which may well be the most controversial yet. As you read on, remember to allow yourself to think through what is being presented and to avoid reacting out of fear and old habit. This is the biggest and most difficult link in the chain to be broken, but if it is not addressed, many of you will never, ever be free.

Part Four

THE
"D"
WORD

I remember my parents' exasperation when I told them I was going to get a divorce. My mother's comment was, "How could you do this to us?"

My brother also confronted me with, "Why did you marry him, then?"

What struck me in that moment was the preposterousness that others take the insult of someone else's divorce on themselves, worrying about their own emotions and what others will think of them or the family rather than acknowledging the pain and turmoil of the divorcing persons. Despite the fact that I was the one who had been lied to, neglected and abused in the marriage, I was somehow made to feel guilty for its failure because I was the one officially ending it.

No one gets married with the intent to divorce unless, of course, they are doing it simply to obtain permanent residency or citizenship in another country! Even women that experience doubt on their wedding day tend to push their apprehensions aside and go through with the ceremony with full intentions of making it work. People seek the ideal in their marriage and believe for the ideal. Unfortunately, the ideal does not always happen and that is why there is divorce.

I know that some of you are thinking, "No marriage is ever ideal, but when you take your vows you are promising to make it work despite the imperfections." While that is a true and noble response, it is also true that in order for differences and problems to be effectively worked through within a marriage certain factors need to be in place.

First of all, it takes the co-operation and effort of both partners. We have all seen examples of how one partner, either the man or the woman, does everything in their power to make things work while the other person puts little or no required effort into the process. This brings us back to the principle of free will. The person who is acting alone to make a marriage work is like someone dragging a dead body along on their journey. Eventually the weight and sorrow of the burden become too much and the person doing the pulling will either have to let that burden go or they will also perish as an individual.

Sometimes the couple encounters problems or difficulties that were impossible to foresee and end up having dreadful consequences to their relationship. This could be anything from outside family interferences to the death of a child. Whether due to personal fear or weakness, immaturity, even personality, one or both of the partners cannot or will not adjust, and eventually life becomes unbearable under such circumstances.

It is for such reasons and others less noble (such as simply wanting to marry someone else for money or lust) that divorce exists. In fact, divorce has coexisted alongside marriage over the history of humankind. As mentioned in our section on marriage, as far back as ancient times a man could traditionally take a wife by three ways: purchase, contract or by having sex with her. Therefore, it took a mere reversal of these actions to put away one's wife, usually in the presence of witnesses. Although the practice and purposes of divorce have varied throughout time and between cultures, there are two basic characteristics of divorce that have always stood out: stigma and power.

Divorce has always carried with it some sort of stigma. Regardless of the reasons or motives for divorce, there has always been an implication of fault or failure, an implication that unfortunately has traditionally fallen on the wife. For example, in ancient times it was considered acceptable and even reasonable for a man to dismiss one wife and replace her with another who could fulfill a particular purpose that his first wife could not, such as to bear children or to gain wealth. Therefore, even if the first wife carried out her marital duties ideally, and even if she was sent away through no fault of her own (i.e. her husband simply desired a better political marriage alliance), she still bore the stigma of having been rejected and put away. To this day divorce still seems to stain the individual, regardless of the reasons for it.

In ancient times divorce was an issue primarily of power, not emotion. Since men have traditionally held that power, divorce was a method and a tool for them to get what they wanted. Since ancient times the power of a man has been expressed in his possession and maintenance of certain key areas: property, progeny and prestige, and because women and children have traditionally been considered to be, at least in part, a form of male property, a man had every right to treat them the same way he would a piece of land, especially if it affected his prestige. This underlying attitude has prevailed throughout history despite some progressive changes, and it still affects and influences the way divorce settlements or issues are viewed. For example, many men who are divorced do not see why they should pay spousal or child support if their family is not living with him. They carry the same mindset that has existed over thousands of years: a wife and children are property; therefore, having to surrender control over them financially or socially is an affront to their male ego, a sign that they no longer have control of what they deemed to be theirs. As a result, divorce has historically been looked upon negatively simply because it represents failure; either failure on the woman's part to somehow please or gratify her husband in some way or another, or the failure of the man to maintain control over his wife and children.

Although stigma and power appear to be intrinsic to the issue of divorce throughout history, the purposes for its creation have varied from culture to culture. In fact, two of the greatest errors in mainstream western civilization are the presumptions that divorce represents the same thing to people everywhere and that it has always been that way. This applies especially to the interpretations the church has formulated over the centuries. Yet, like the marriage covenant, divorce during ancient biblical times had a unique and deliberate purpose that corresponded perfectly to the culture and mindset of its day. In fact, divorce in the Old Testament and first century Christianity was different in form and purpose to our modern day divorce.

Bible scholar Spiros Zodhiates, whose expertise is in exegeses and word origins of both biblical Hebrew and Greek, points out that the biblical bill of divorcement or *get* should not be equated with our modern day divorce, the purpose of which is simply to dissolve a marital union.[36] Instead, the bill of divorcement was designed to absolve an innocent spouse of otherwise presumed fault or guilt, thereby releasing them to remarry without stigma. This is largely unknown by most of the population, especially Christians, who have been taught that divorce is a sin, period.

The removal of divorce from its original and proper purpose in the biblical context has resulted in confusion and centuries of condemnation against those who desperately needed to leave spouses who abused and rejected them. That reason alone is enough to go back to the beginning, as we did with the marriage covenant, to put back into proper perspective the role of divorce among the faithful.

Because of the depth of controversy of the subject, we need to examine in detail the scriptures that mention divorce as well as the cultural background. The author therefore begs the reader's patience for the depth of study and discussion on the subject. I feel, however, that this is essential if it is going to free anyone's mind once and for all. Again, keep in mind as these points are discussed that I am not talking about modern day, western civilization divorce as we know it but divorce from the biblical perspective set in its original and proper context. After we have examined divorce in biblical context, it will shed new light on our attitude toward divorce in our modern culture.

We will be looking at divorce from the perspective of both Jewish and Christian Scriptures, centering on three places: the Law or *Torah* (the first five books of what Christians call the Old Testament), the Gospel accounts (centering around the life and ministry of Jesus), and the Epistles (letters attributed to Paul of Tarsus as found in the latter sections of the New Testament). Although divorce is mentioned in other places, such as the Prophets, we will concentrate on these three sections since this is where divorce is mentioned in an instructive context. We will begin with a look at the Old Testament and continue our discussion into the New Testament. Dividing the topic into specific parts is necessary not only because of the sheer amount of information that we are required to analyze, but it also helps us focus on what was happening at each particular point in history when these instructions were written. Because the scriptures in the New Testament are built on ones from the Old Testament you will notice that some of these intertwine and appear to be repetitive in some places.

Divorce in the Old Testament

The very first reference to divorce in the Bible is found in the Old Testament in Deuteronomy 24:1–4a:

> *When a man takes a wife and marries her, and it happens that she finds no favor in his eyes because he has found some uncleanness in her[5], and he writes her a certificate of divorce, puts it in her hand, and sends her out of his house, when she has departed from his house, and goes and becomes another man's wife, if the latter husband detests her and writes her a certificate of divorce, puts it in her hand, and sends her out of his house, or if the latter husband dies who took her to be his wife, then her former husband who divorced her must not take her back to be his wife…*

Now, let us draw out the relevant points. First, note that the verses apply to the man and not the woman. There is a reason for this. During ancient times only men had the right to instigate divorce.

---

[5] The *Complete Jewish Bible* reads: "*…finds* [something about] *her* [that is] *displeasing, because he has found her offensive in some respect…*". This is relevant considering where our discussion will take us further on.

That is why divorce was also referred to as a "sending away of a wife." This solid power began to change within Judaism from the year 1000, when Rabbenu Gershom decreed that a woman could challenge being "automatically" sent away and divorced against her will (unless she committed adultery, in which case divorce was and still is automatically granted). Although a man could more easily send his wife away, if a woman wanted to leave her marriage she was forced to appeal to a higher authority in order to persuade them to force her husband to free her. In ancient times such an opportunity rarely existed. There is evidence within Judaism, however, that if a man divorced his wife and remarried and it was discovered later that they had carried out an extra-marital affair previous to his divorce, the new marriage was automatically dissolved as a sign of disgust and judicial unfairness against the first wife.[37] Otherwise, the lack of power on the wife's part meant that women were helpless if their husbands simply wanted to cast them away.

The second point we see from these verses is that they are written in the style of direct, legal instruction. For example, the phrases "and he writes her a certificate of divorce" and "when she has departed from his house, and goes and becomes another man's wife" are statements without prejudice, meaning they carry no moral accusation with them. In other words, there is no direct or insinuated condemnation either of the existence or deliverance of the bill of divorcement or of remarriage. This is because this was well known and standard practice. That is not to say, however, that divorce for any reason was acceptable either, and this brings us to our next point.

In order for a man to be justified in putting away his wife there had to be something that he found displeasing or offensive in her. The word is often translated as "unclean." Christians usually presume this to mean sin, yet in Jewish culture things or people are not deemed as unclean only because of sin. For example, touching a dead body, even to prepare it for burial, made one unclean. A woman is considered unclean when she is menstruating, but that does not mean she is sinful. In fact, there is so much meaning behind the word translated as "unclean" that we will discuss it in detail further down.

Aside from having just cause to put his wife away, the only other directive was that the man was forbidden to take back his former wife after she had remarried and was then sent away by that husband or widowed. This is a very interesting point since some Christian sects teach that people who have remarried should divorce their current spouse and return to their first one in order to "undo" the sin of their divorce and remarriage, obviously overlooking the above scripture. Since the majority of Christians have been taught that divorce and remarriage are always sins, this may be confusing for readers. Bear with me. The more we examine these Scriptures in their proper cultural and historical context, the more you will understand them.

As stated above, when a man sent away his wife he was commanded to provide her with a bill of divorcement, also known as a *get*. The bill represented a total cutting off between a man and his wife. It was therefore a declaration that the marriage was irreparably broken down. This did two things: first, it granted permission to the released woman to remarry; and secondly, it absolved her of any suspicion or guilt of adultery in the eyes of others. In other words, if a man did not give the woman such a bill it could be presumed that she had committed adultery. During the time of the writing of this law, adultery was punishable by stoning. Such a bill would therefore be rendered useless to an unfaithful wife since she would not be alive for long anyway! However, according to the Law, both the man as well as the woman guilty of adultery had to be stoned (Leviticus 20:10). This implies that those guilty of adultery would have been caught in the act since no one could be condemned without the testimony of witnesses. In other words, if no witnesses could be brought forth, or if the man that the woman was supposedly sleeping with was also not identified, the woman alone could not be put to death. This was to avoid the carrying out of horrible consequences on those who might be falsely accused.[38]

Nonetheless, let us presume that a woman was sent away by her husband without a bill of divorcement but also that there was no evidence to tie her to adultery. She would still be under suspicion of having committed adultery. Moreover, since a bill of divorcement declared a woman no longer legally bound to her husband, a woman who was sent away without such a document would still be considered legally tied to him, even if he had already sent her away. As a result, she would be considered to be committing adultery should she remarry, and the man with her would be considered an adulterer. The bill was essential, therefore, not only to absolve a woman from the accusation of adultery but also to free her to marry again without stigma. That is why there is such emphasis for the man to place the bill of divorcement into the hands of the wife he is sending away.

The other emphasis is on the reason a man sends his wife away. He must have justifiable cause, and that cause included some type of fault within the woman. From this wording it appears that only women are targeted for fault. However, given that at the time of writing only men could initiate divorce, this draws out the fact that a man had to have good and just cause for dismissing his wife. Since women were unable to initiate divorce at this time, it would be redundant to draw out fault on the opposite side. The objective, rather, was so that men would not lightly dismiss a wife since in those times a woman's sustenance was tied directly to their relationship with men.

A woman usually only lived in her father's or her husband's house (unless she was a bondservant, in which case she lived in her master's household). If she became widowed, either one of her husband's brothers would marry her (levirate marriage) or she could continue to live on her dead husband's property and earn money from skills or selling things, perhaps also getting help from other family members. However, if she was sent away she would only have the following choices for economic survival: she would either be forced to return to her father's home and he would resume providing for her, or she would have to remarry in order for another man to support her. This, incidentally, is the very reason remarriage was not only acceptable, but in most cases, necessary. If those choices were not possible—if for example her father was no longer alive and no other male relative was able or willing to take her in, or if the ancestral property had been taken over for debt or confiscated, or if she could not find another man to marry her (a likelihood especially if she was accused, even falsely, of being an adulteress)—she would either be forced into prostitution or risk being sold into slavery for outstanding debt. This clause in Scripture, therefore, was meant to protect women against cruel and unjustified rejection and to prevent them from a life of extreme hardship and sin. The bill of divorcement, then, was actually a good thing, meant to keep them from a fate over which they had no personal control.

Given the potential for women to end up in dire economic and personal situations, the only reason given in the Torah that justified a man to put away his wife was that there had to be something so disagreeable about her that he simply could not bring himself to continue living with her, even to the extent that there was no hope of reconciliation. That "something" has been the source of debate throughout Judaism even to this day. So, what was that "something"? Although it is translated as "uncleanness" in the above passage and others, in Hebrew it is *ervat davar*, with the generally agreed-upon translation by rabbis as 'a matter (or thing) of indecency.' The debate lies in what exactly is meant by the word "indecency."

This same debate was raging at the time of Jesus of Nazareth, and this is strongly reflected in the Gospels. The opposite viewpoints of exactly what *ervat davar* meant were represented by two rabbinical schools of thought at the time, Bet Hillel and Bet Shammai. Bet Hillel believed that divorce was permitted if the man found *any* indecent thing about his wife, the "thing" (davar) being at the discretion of the husband (so arose the cynical assertion that a man could divorce his wife for burning the toast!). To be fair, however, I do not believe that something as serious as divorce would be taken so lightly in the eyes of Judaism. In fact, the Talmud states that "the very altar weeps for one who divorces the wife of his youth."[39] To the school of Hillel, therefore, the matter of indecency was anything that caused friction in the home to the point where the marital relationship between the man and his wife was disrupted and violated on a daily basis.[40]

Bet Shammai, on the other hand, focused on the word *erva* (in the grammatical form of the sentence as *ervat*). Interestingly, that word refers to the genitals, and that could be the reason why Bet Shammai held that a man must not divorce his wife unless she had committed some sort of sexual transgression or had some manner of sexual indecency about her.

Most presume this to mean adultery; however, as we have just seen, it was unlikely that a bill or *get* would be given to a woman guilty of adultery, and there was a very real possibility of death by stoning at the time of its original writing. By reason of deduction, therefore, that matter of indecency could not have been adultery. In other words, if it meant adultery, God would have just simply had it written as adultery! That is precisely why the debate continues to this day, because its interpretation is not a literal one.

Now I am about to go out on a limb with my own theory about the meaning based on various rabbinical opinions. If the word *erva* is a reference to genitals yet does not fit into the context of adultery, then it must represent something else that is considered to be related to genitals other than sexual intercourse (since intercourse in this context would only be considered a violation if done with someone other than one's spouse).

Let us look at the context and attitude of ancient Judaism. The genitals represent intimacy, and that intimacy is restricted between certain individuals. This is outlined within the laws regarding sexual morality in Chapter 18 of Leviticus where it refers to sexual and intimate relationships. Interestingly, the phraseology used to describe both *intention* of sexual contact as well as the act itself is written as "uncovering the nakedness of" someone else. This makes sense since there must be exposure or uncovering of the genitals in order to have sexual relations. Therefore, one's "nakedness" or "genitals" refers to a type of relationship unique only to those involved in it. In fact, a Hebrew idiom which means to have sex with someone is to intimately "know" them. In Chapter 18 of Leviticus not all incestuous or illicit acts are specified; they are simply represented by the term "uncover the nakedness of." Why would someone (especially in those days) uncover another person? Since exposing someone's nakedness or uncovering them would only occur if there was the intention of sexual relations, that would make intention as important or incriminating as the act itself. This implies, therefore, that intimacy, illicit or moral, begins with the intentions of the heart and mind.

The other important feature of "nakedness" in Leviticus is that it is described as being owned by either the person who is being exposed or individuals with whom they have legitimate relationships with, such as a husband or wife.[41] Again, this implies intimacy and "rights" to that intimacy, and that level of intimacy is represented in one key area of the body, the genitals. Therefore, I believe that *ervat davar* refers to something that only a husband and wife could know about each other because of their level of intimacy. Since we also know that it cannot mean adultery, we are left with a wide open field of meaning. That is why the rabbis do not want to pinpoint only one interpretation to it—because by virtue of the way it is written, one cannot! In other words, it can simply mean that if a man should uncover something that he finds repulsive about his wife, something so repulsive that she loses favor in his sight (respect or affection) to the point that he can no longer stand to live with her—and more importantly, sleep with her—then he can or must release her. Remember that conjugal rights or *ona* is a requirement of the marriage covenant; therefore, if a man neglects his wife's sexual needs because he disdains her for some personal reason, then he is obligated to let her go. To this day, a man's neglect to be intimate with his wife is unquestionable grounds for divorce. However, since the personal issue between the husband and wife affects only him, she is free to remarry.

At this point I feel I need to address Christians here specifically, because confusion often arises from wrongful interpretations of the Law. Some Christians believe that God would never permit divorce, that it is a sin, period. When faced with these Old Testament scriptures they usually use one of two arguments: that Jesus disqualified or did away with the Law, or that Moses "added" his opinion to the Law and therefore it can be flawed. Neither argument applies. First, Jesus specifically said that he did not come to do away with the Law but to fulfill it. Secondly, we cannot presume error on Moses' part because God himself states that Moses was unique from other prophets in that he was the only one with whom God spoke directly. In Numbers 12:8 it says, "I speak with him face to face, even plainly, and not in dark sayings; and he sees the form of the Lord. Why then were you not afraid to speak against My servant Moses?" If God wanted to make sure that people knew His will it would make sense that He would then speak to Moses directly in order for His words to be recorded accurately. It is therefore inaccurate to presume

RELEASING THE CAPTIVE WOMAN

that what Moses said or wrote is either irrelevant or even different than the will of God. So if Moses did not make up the law concerning divorce in the Old Testament but simply wrote down what God told him, we need to ask ourselves a very important question: whose idea was the bill of divorcement?

To sum up what we have already learned, divorce was initially and intentionally meant to protect women from unjustly being sent away with no means of provision. To the woman who was not guilty of adultery it exonerated her reputation, leaving her free to remarry. A woman who was unable to remarry or had no male relative who was willing or able to take her in had no choice but to earn her living through prostitution or slavery. The bill of divorcement, then, was not only meant to exonerate the woman but to keep her from a life of misery and sin.

Divorce in the Gospel Accounts

Reasons for divorce or putting away one's wife was a hot topic in Jesus' day. Why is this? We have already learned that the rights of women in Judaism during the time of Jesus were already beginning to be adversely affected through the infiltration of other cultural influences that were less sympathetic in their viewpoint of women. Since the only justification in Judaism according to the Law for sending a wife away was to claim some despicable thing about her, arguments arose as to just what that meant.

The Gospels give some of the most detailed insight into the argument of the day between Bet Hillel and Bet Shammai in regards to divorce. Although the actual "schools" of Hillel and Shammai are not directly mentioned in the Gospels, their differing viewpoints are—especially in the dialogue between Jesus, his disciples, and some of the Pharisees.

Luke 16:1–18 records Jesus giving a parable about a master and a steward, and then, seemingly out of the blue, he ends his discourse with a statement about divorce that does not seem to fit the context. For the sake of space, we will only quote from verse 14 onward, but I recommend that you find a New Testament and read the entire context for yourself:

Now the Pharisees, who were lovers of money, also heard all these things [just said about the master and the steward], and they derided Him.[6] And He said to them, "You are those who justify yourselves before men, but God knows your hearts. For what is highly esteemed among men is an abomination in the sight of God.

The law and the prophets were until John. Since that time the kingdom of God has been preached, and everyone is pressing into it. And it is easier for heaven and earth to pass away than for one tittle of the law to fail. Whoever divorces his wife and marries another commits adultery; and whoever marries her who is divorced from her husband commits adultery.

Is it a mistake to suddenly have a verse about divorce stuck in there at the end, seemingly out of context? No it is not. In examining any document or recording, we need to look at a few critical rules, one of which is looking first at to whom the statement is being addressed and the context in which it is written. After Jesus' teaching on stewardship and faithfulness, verse 14 states that some particular Pharisees, the ones who loved money and the prestigious image it gave them, were angry about his comments. Jesus' response is interesting. He points out that (and I am paraphrasing here) no matter what we do or how we interpret the Law for ourselves, what is written is written and nothing in the universe can ever change it. It is immediately after this point that he sticks in the comment about a man divorcing his wife and marrying another, or, to be more specific, in order to marry another.

---

[6] The way the Bible is written in its original form, there were no punctuations such as commas, etc. Because of the increase of anti-Semitism within Christianity over the ages, a convenient "comma" was placed in this verse so that rather than reading "the Pharisees who loved money" it says, "the Pharisees, who loved money…" giving the implication that *all* Pharisees were lovers of money. Let us remember, however, that some Pharisees were supporters of Jesus. We must also note here that there were different sects or "denominations" of belief then as there are now. For example, the Sadducees did not believe in the spiritual realm. It doesn't make sense, then, to label one entire group in a negative light. To this day, even among Christians there are various denominations who disagree on various points. The focus in this verse is therefore on the particular Pharisee individuals who were greedy and whose motives were the love of money, and not on the Pharisees collectively. This type of attitude has only bred and justified anti-Semitism and prohibited unity between Jew and Christian.

The Gospels were written in koine Greek. The phrase "and marries another" uses the word *kai* for "and" and *heteros* for "another." This is interesting because according to Zhodiates, *kai* has a "copulative and sometimes also a cumulative force." In other words, it is meant to connect two phrases or references in the context.[42] Hence, the previous action is tied directly to the second action. The choice for the word "another" is also interesting. There were at least two options in the Greek: *heteros*, a reference to quality; and *allos*, which usually refers to numbers or quantity as opposed to quality.[43] In English we are not used to such specific word choice, yet this was common in ancient languages and is still in existence in some modern dialects. The point here is that particular words were used in order to get a specific message across. Translated in that context, the phrase "divorces his wife and marries another" refers, then, to the fact that these men were divorcing their wives with the purpose or intent to specifically marry another person, and for "qualitative" reasons—in other words, someone who in their eyes was better than the woman they were currently married to. As mentioned earlier in the book, this could have been for political and economic reasons, a practice common among the Romans and Greeks and perhaps infiltrating into Judaic culture. This possibility could be further supported by the context of Jesus' reference to things that are esteemed by men. The other possibility is that the qualitative reason could have simply been lust.

As just mentioned, Jesus begins his teaching by telling a story about a master and steward. Based on what we learned from the marriage covenant, the husband's role as the "greater" partner could be equated with that of a master (as provider) and the role of the wife (who is entrusted with looking after the master's household) as that of steward. In the story, the master unjustly puts away his faithful steward (it is necessary at this point to mention that the way it is translated gives the impression that the steward was "unjust," however, according to Zodiates and other scholars it should be interpreted as "unjustly treated"). This could be why Jesus made a direct analogy between the two in his discourse, that is, between master and servant and husband and wife.

He uses this parable to demonstrate how putting away one's current wife for no other reason than to acquire another wife ought to be considered as unfair and cruel as a master who wrongfully dismisses a faithful steward. The implications of this were serious when we look at it from the cultural perspective of the time. No person would ever hire a steward with a stained reputation. In the same way, the dismissed wife would also have a stained reputation by implication of the fact that she had been sent away. In each case, both the steward and the rejected wife would end up personally and economically destitute and desperate.

Jesus then brings in another interesting element. He sums up his discourse with the statement that a man who puts away his wife and marries another commits adultery. This is interesting since, according to the verses in Deuteronomy regarding divorce, adultery on the man's part is not even mentioned. This is not to say that men do not nor will not commit adultery but rather it is presumed that the man's reasons for sending away his wife are justified and that his intentions are pure.

For some, the fact that Jesus includes men as potential adulterers in his teachings causes them to think that he was doing away with the traditional interpretation of the Law, perhaps even creating a new standard. Let us see if that is the case.

Jesus distinctly says that he did not come to destroy the Law but to fulfill it (Matthew 5:17). Again, going back to the use of particular words in the Greek, the expression here "to fulfill" means "to enforce [something that already exists] and explain it fully."[44] So we know from this statement that Jesus was not inventing a new standard. As mentioned earlier in the book, Judaism has traditionally looked down upon the practice of doing away with one's current wife simply to marry another woman of preference. Recall also our recent discussion on "ervat davar" which led us back to the Leviticus chapter on "uncovering the nakedness" of another whom you are not permitted to uncover. Remember that such phraseology not only dealt with actual sexual encounters but also and especially *the intent of the heart and mind* (see p. 68). Jesus reiterates this point very, very clearly as recorded in Matthew 5:27–28:

> *You have heard that it was said to those of old, "You shall not commit*
> *adultery." But I say to you that whoever looks at a woman to lust for*
> *her has already committed adultery with her in his heart.*

It would appear therefore, that Jesus was not setting a new precedent but was in fact reinforcing the full purpose of the original standard that these men were walking away from. This is reaffirmed in his discourse on divorce in Matthew 5, verses 31–32:

> *Furthermore it has been said, "Whoever divorces his wife, let him*
> *give her a certificate of divorce." But I say to you that whoever*
> *divorces his wife* for any reason *except sexual immorality* [ervat
> davar] *causes her to commit adultery; and whoever marries a*
> *woman who is divorced commits adultery.* (emphasis mine)

The above statement not only rebukes the men of the time for unjustifiably sending away their wives, there is evidence that they were doing so in such a way as to make her look like an adulteress so that anyone marrying her later would also be labeled an adulterer. This could only happen in a number of ways. As we already discussed, if a man sent his wife away without a *get*, it was presumed she committed adultery. We also know that the only way she would not be stoned to death was if there were no witnesses to the adultery and/or if the man she supposedly committed adultery with was not brought forth as well.

There was also another reason why a woman could not be stoned to death for adultery, and that was because under Roman rule the Jews in Judea could only put another Jew to death for violation of religious law under the power of the civil authority of Rome.[45] These elements are strongly reflected in the story of the woman supposedly *caught* in adultery in The Gospel of John, chapter 8. In this account, some elders present a woman to Jesus whom they say was caught in the act. They question him, stating that according to the Law she should be put to death, but then they ask him what he thinks. The text states that they presented this situation to Jesus to deliberately test him.

Now, I know a lot of Christians think that Jesus' response of "whoever is without sin, let him cast the first stone" was a lesson on not judging other people, which again could be taken as him setting another precedent; however, there is more to the story than that. Let us presume that Jesus was being tested. If the Law stated that an adulteress should be stoned, would Jesus be doing away with the Law by releasing her? Again, the Law states that both the man and the woman guilty of adultery must be brought forward for judgment; so Jesus could have had this in mind in not condemning her since only she was brought forth.

I believe, however, that a more important aspect was in place here, and that was where Jesus' loyalties lay. If he agreed that she should be stoned to death (with the premise that the guilty man should also be brought forth), they could accuse him to the Romans of disrespecting or even planning to break Roman law. However, if he would have outwardly said as much, they could then accuse him of being a Roman loyalist. The question then was: would he be loyal to the Law of God or to the law of the Romans? One of the reasons I believe this to be the main issue is that similar testing is mentioned in other areas of the Gospels, where Jesus is asked whether to obey God or Roman authority.[46] Perhaps that is why Jesus does not answer either way, except to write certain things in the dirt and to respond that whoever is without sin should cast the first stone. These men knew perfectly well that they were being underhanded, perhaps even setting this woman up, and so they dropped the matter. Who knows, maybe their names were being written in the dirt?

The Gospels, therefore, paint a picture of the conditions that not only surrounded the argument of just what justified a man to divorce his wife but also the manner in which it was done. From these texts, as well as the historical fact that the *ketubah* mentioned earlier (a marriage contract which made it very difficult for a man to divorce his wife) had already been introduced by Jesus' day and was gaining ground, tells us that wives were being unjustly dumped because their husbands lusted after other women.

Another possibility is that some men were actually divorcing their wives *and* giving her a bill of divorcement even if their reasons for doing so did not follow the Law. In other words, they thought that as long as they followed the letter of the Law by putting a bill of divorcement in her hand, it was all right. This is where the arguments from the school of Hillel could have been used (perhaps misused) as grounds for justification for sending one's wife away, as Jesus pointed out, *for any reason*. Again, it is not the divorce itself nor the bill of divorcement that is condemned but the motives behind it. Let us examine another Gospel account that backs this up:

> *The Pharisees came and asked Him, "Is it lawful for a man to divorce his wife?" testing Him.*
>
> *And He answered and said to them, "What did Moses command you?" They said, "Moses permitted a man to write a certificate of divorce, and to dismiss her."*
>
> *And Jesus answered and said to them, "Because of the hardness of your heart he wrote you this precept. But from the beginning of the creation, God 'made them male and female'. 'For this reason a man shall leave his father and mother and be joined to his wife, and the two shall become one flesh'; so then they are no longer two, but one flesh. Therefore what God has joined together let not man separate."*
>
> *In the house His disciples also asked Him again about the same matter. So He said to them, "Whoever divorces his wife and marries* another *commits adultery against her* [emphasis mine: recall the previous discussion on this phrase]. *And if a woman divorces her husband and marries another, she commits adultery."* (Mark 10:2–12)

Here we see that some men—who Jesus obviously targeted for unlawfully and immorally dumping their wives in order to marry someone else—again attempt to test him, this time on the issue of divorce. In asking him whether it is lawful to divorce a wife, they know that if he says "yes" they could then accuse him of condemning them for divorcing. A good way to respond to those who are testing you is to answer their question with a question, and Jesus does just that. He asks, "What did Moses command you?" Now note the men's response. They point out that Moses instructed them to give their wife a bill of divorcement when releasing her, referring to the verses we looked at in Deuteronomy at the beginning of this section, but they also leave out the fact that they should be justified in doing so. Jesus then draws attention to the initial purpose of the bill of divorcement as a means of protecting women from being unjustly dumped, directly stating that the provision of divorce was established because of the hardness of men's hearts. In other words, there will be husbands who God knows will not do what they are supposed to do because of selfishness and stubbornness. A pliable heart is willing to change and see things differently, even to soften; a hard heart is immovable, defiant and never admits fault. Knowing that such men would exist, God therefore made provision not only to protect women from being unjustly abandoned and dumped but also to be released from a life of personal misery.

In Judaism, sexual immorality and adultery were regarded as absolute and undisputed reasons for divorce (after and during the time the death penalty for adultery disappeared).[47] It was also permitted in cases of impotence, when a man could not meet the provision of procreation or sexual gratification for his wife; if he was personally or hygienically filthy; or if he forced his wife to do things she was not only not obliged to but that violated her personally as well.[48] These tenets stand to this day. However, even though there has always been an acceptance of divorce within both ancient and contemporary Judaism, this does not mean that divorce is taken lightly. In fact, the traditional Judaic viewpoint is that although divorce is permitted it is also "morally reprehensible."[49] Yet the reality that there will always be people who use and abuse others, especially those with less power than themselves, has also not been neglected. For this reason Judaism has traditionally attempted to provide a way out for women who find themselves in unbearable marital situations.

For example, a woman with a complaint could approach a council of spiritual leaders or a rabbi and request help. The desired result would be that the woman's husband would be held accountable by that authority with an expectation that he would change. If he refused, he could be made to let her go rather than chain her to a life of misery. Although not in every case, especially in some more orthodox circles where men still traditionally hold a tight rein, Judaism has leaned more toward the woman's side: "If there is a doubt as to the originator of the quarrel, the husband is not believed when he asserts that the wife has commenced the dispute, as all women are presumed to be lovers of domestic peace."[50] As Jesus agreed, "your hearts are hard." The ideal, of course, is that all difficulties within the marriage be resolved as outlined in the verses from Genesis as quoted by Jesus. The Shulchan Aruch thus exhorts rabbis to exhaust every possible means to discourage a husband and wife from divorcing.

The Genesis verses quoted by Jesus to these men represent, again, the original will of God and the standard of perfection. The ideal is for a man and a woman to be so united and complete in each other that they should become as one. If, indeed, God has truly put a certain man and woman together, then no one should seek to interfere with that relationship, and I strongly presume that to include would-be adulterers. We can put it this way: Thou shall not covet thy neighbor's wife. One can also not help but notice that a particular command is given to leaving one's parents, a suggestion perhaps that parents and in-laws may also be the most likely of potential marriage destroyers. Although we can chuckle at the reference here, there is definitely truth to this. Certainly adult children should continue showing respect for their parents; yet it is also true that many marriages have gone on the rocks because of family interference. Even two people who are perfectly matched can have their relationship destroyed by others. In fact, when there is no familial love, support and acceptance from the in-laws, especially toward the wife—and more importantly, if the husband does not put a stop to the criticisms (or cleave to his wife)—the marriage is truly jeopardized.

So in these passages Jesus is making it clear to these men that by divorcing their wives for the sole purpose of marrying another they are actually committing adultery. This point makes sense, for if their intentions were pure and they were justified according to the Law for putting away their wives, adultery would not even be mentioned in the verse. The fact that it is mentioned confirms that the intention of these men in divorcing their wives was simply to go after a "better" catch and not because the first wife had violated her part in the marriage. Through these statements Jesus establishes the fact of their misuse of the bill of divorcement and the Law.

In the final verse, Jesus makes another interesting statement: "… if a woman divorces her husband and marries another, she commits adultery" (Mark 10:12). This last verse is a challenge since it presents a contradiction to the practice of the times. The difficulty comes from the statement of *the wife divorcing the husband*. Remember that in those days it was literally impossible for women to divorce their husbands; they simply had no legal means to do so. There are at least three conclusions that can account for this inconsistency: 1) Jesus set a different standard, albeit moral; 2) the Gospels are historically inaccurate; or 3) there has been a mistranslation. With regard to the first conclusion, I really do not think that Jesus could not have known and understood the religious and civil restrictions of his own day. Even if he wanted to establish a different moral standard, what would be the point if there was already a legal impossibility for a woman to initiate divorce?

So, could the Gospels be historically inaccurate? Any ancient document or work always has that possibility; however, there are too many other facts documented within the Gospels that back up their historical authenticity. Also, no one concocting a story would make such a blatant cultural and historical error, especially one that would jeopardize its credibility. I realize that some do not trust the Gospels as historical documents simply because they disagree with its message; however, whether or not we agree with the contents of historical documents or texts does not mean they are not legitimate.

Given that, we need to look at the third possibility—that some error was made in the translation or interpretation of the text. After all, the Gospels are some of the most recopied of historical texts with several different "types" of translations. It does not seem unreasonable, then, that misconceptions of culture or history, even misapplications of terminology, could occur over the passage of time.

When we think of divorce in our modern minds, we think of a legal process in which both a man and a woman agree to end their marital union, and although divorce today still requires justifiable grounds, the attitude remains that it is the divorce itself that ends that marriage.

To the ancient mind, however, the process of divorce simply reflected what had already occurred—that is, the breaking of the terms of the marital contract or covenant. In other words, to the modern mind divorce ends the marriage, to the ancient mind violating marital terms that had been agreed upon ends the marriage and divorce is simply the final representation of that fact. Also remember that the ancient divorce was described as a sending away of a *wife* since only men had the legal authority to instigate it. The translation in this verse, then, cannot refer to divorce itself but to something else that created the death of the marriage such as a form of abandonment of one's husband. In other words, even though a woman could not "put away" her husband legally she could still do so circumstantially by simply leaving him. In fact, the Greek word used in the text not only refers to this, it also has the connotation of *allowing* someone to depart.[51] Could this also mean, then, that a woman whose husband was attempting to dump her for another woman should, in the eyes of Jesus, hold her husband both personally and outwardly accountable for his behavior instead of groveling for his affection and approval?

In either case it is evident from the Gospels that some men were either twisting the Law or ignoring it altogether so that they could divorce their wives in order to marry others. We have also seen that this change of attitude toward wives in general seems to have seeped in from the dominant cultures of the time: the Romans and the Greeks. This is further substantiated by other parts of the New Testament, including the letters written by the apostle Paul to the Greek and Roman converts to the new faith. This brings us to our final look at divorce in Scripture, the Pauline letters.

DIVORCE ACCORDING TO PAUL

As we have just learned, divorce in the ancient world could not be instigated by women. Despite this fact we come across the same terminology within Paul's writings as we have just discussed in the last Gospel account—that is, a command for a woman not to divorce her husband. There are other interesting factors in Paul's instructions, some which appear to differ yet again from the Law and the Gospels. Let us take a look at the key instructive verses in their entirety and then analyze them in light of their historical and cultural background:

Now to the married I command, yet not I but the Lord: A wife is not to depart from her husband. But even if she does depart, let her remain unmarried or be reconciled to her husband. And a husband is not to divorce his wife.

But to the rest I, not the Lord, say: If any brother has a wife who does not believe, and she is willing to live with him, let him not divorce her. And a woman who has a husband who does not believe, if he is willing to live with her, let her not divorce him [emphasis mine]. *For the unbelieving husband is sanctified by the wife, and the unbelieving wife is sanctified by the husband; otherwise your children would be unclean, but now they are holy. But if the unbeliever departs, let him depart; a brother or sister is not under bondage in such cases. But God has called us to peace. For how do you know, O wife, whether you will save your husband? Or how do you know, O husband, whether you will save your wife?* (1 Corinthians 7:10–16)

At a glance it appears that Paul is somewhat more restrictive in his approach regarding separation and divorce in marriage, yet he was a Jew, as Jesus was, raised within the tenets of Judaism. Remember that, despite disagreements among Jews, early Christianity was still considered a sect of Judaism in its early days, and that meant for Paul there was no difference in his knowledge, attitude and approach toward things such as the marital covenant. If the Law as well as the teachings of Jesus allowed for divorce under certain circumstances, why does it appear that Paul does not? The short answer: because of the civil and cultural restrictions and realities in which his audience lived in. Now the long answer …

First of all, Paul is addressing Gentiles—more specifically in this case, Greeks—people who had no personal knowledge or experience of the Law of Moses. This also explains why the majority of the letters (a.k.a. epistles) retained in the New Testament are instructive in nature, at times going into detail regarding certain customs or practices stemming from a Judaic foundation. Sometimes Paul even states that his purpose in writing is in response to some of their questions. If Paul had been addressing people who were already acquainted with Judaic customs and culture, there would have been no need for him to do this. In other words, Paul is trying to make the tenets of this new religion fit into a Gentile backdrop, a backdrop which often severely contradicted the Judaic mindset and practices, particularly in terms of moral allowances. This was especially so in regards to sexuality and marriage, and that is why such topics tend to dominate his letters to the Corinthians.

The second point stems from the first, and that is that Paul is addressing individuals whom he considers to have adopted a belief in the God of the Bible as opposed to their previous adherence to polytheism. It is in that light that Paul instructs them in regards to covenantal relationship as laid out in the Law and the Prophets. Remember that there was no "New Testament" then, and so the main source of religious instruction and teaching of the time, especially concerning the practical issues of life such as marriage and sexuality, was the Tanak, or Jewish Bible. Even in the Tanak there is a distinction made between those who believe in God and those who do not. It is from this same basis that Paul addresses his audience.

A third and essential element to consider is that these Gentile converts were suddenly put in a situation in which their very own upbringing and personal culture not only lacked understanding for their new faith, it was often downright hostile toward it. They did not have the same benefits as Jews whose entire culture was grounded in covenantal relationship. This meant that the Greek converts had no outside support system on which they could rely or to whom they could be held accountable if they needed spiritual guidance. Greek women especially had no equivalent of the Jewish *ketubah* or marriage contract, let alone a bill of divorcement from which they could extract certain rights and protection. Keep in mind also that, in the case of Jewish couples, both the man and the woman were presumed to already be in covenantal relationship with God. In the case of the Greeks, this benefit did not exist among couples in which one of them converted to the new religion while already married. This clashing of cultural and religious practices very much complicated matters for the Greek converts and changed the dynamics of marriage altogether. This is why in the above passages Paul addresses two "types" of married people: in the first section he was speaking to those Greeks in whose relationship both the husband and the wife were believers. Notice, however, in the latter section he refers to "the rest," those being individuals who had converted and now found themselves living with an unbelieving husband or wife. With that in mind, let us look at the verses now in their order.

Paul gives the Greek couples who were both believers the same instruction the Law gives the Jews—that is, God's ideal of a one-man/one-woman covenantal relationship that is meant to last throughout their lifetime. It is the same instruction that Jesus reiterated to his audience from Genesis: what God has put together "let no man put asunder." Paul opens his passage to these married couples by first instructing the women not to depart from their husbands. In fact, he states that this is not his opinion but a command from the Lord, meaning that the tenet is based on the Torah: "And unto the married I command, yet not I, but the Lord, Let not the wife *depart* from her husband: But and if she depart, let her remain unmarried or be reconciled to her husband: and let not the husband *put away* his wife" [KJV, italics mine for emphasis]. The meaning of the word "to depart"—here in reference to the woman leaving—not only means to go away from, but more specifically, "to put asunder." It is the same terminology used by Jesus in his statement: "therefore what God has joined together, let no man put asunder."[52]

Paul, then, was not setting a new standard or moving away from what Jesus taught any more than what Jesus taught was moving away from the Law. "To put asunder" is not simply leaving, it has a more personal, even selfish connotation in this context. It is written in the Middle Voice, a term in grammar that means the subject (in this case, the wife) is acting on or doing something for itself. Not every fine detail is given here, but again, considering that Paul is addressing two believers, there is an expectation on the couple to live within the ideal of Scripture. Taking this into account, it appears that there is no reason for this woman to *have to* leave (i.e. she is not being abused), yet obviously this was happening among the believers or he would not have specifically mentioned it. In fact, the manner in which Paul suddenly brings up certain issues within his letters tells us that he must be responding to inquiries as to what certain people should do under circumstances that are obviously outside their norm.

In the case of this woman, we get the sense that there is no justification for her to leave, thereby making her guilty of violating her marital obligations. Under such circumstances she is not free to remarry for two very good reasons: First, she is not divorced! Her husband has not legally released her and therefore she is still bound to him. She would, therefore, be committing adultery if she went with another man. The second reason has already been stated: there is the strong implication that her departure is unjustified. Since she is neither spiritually nor legally released, Paul naturally instructs her to *remain unmarried* (in other words, she *cannot* marry) or to be reconciled with her husband.

Paul then continues his instruction to the husband of the believing couple to not *put away* his wife (v. 11). The words translated as *put away* are altogether different than the one referring to the woman *departing* from her husband; in fact, it is the equivalent to the translations we discussed earlier and therefore is referring to a man unjustly sending his wife away. We see the same word used further down in Paul's address to "the rest." We know what Paul means by "the rest" because of the specific instructions which follow. Since his letters to the Corinthians are addressed to believers in general, we know then that in this section he is again talking to believers, specifically those who have converted while already married and who now find themselves in a spiritually blended marriage. This is also why Paul tells them that the instruction he is giving them is not according to Torah or "the Lord" but his own interpretation of how such a unique circumstance should be handled. Remember, in those days two Jews marrying were presumed to both be under covenant, and so for Jews to be in a blended marriage (believer/unbeliever) meant they had to have married non-Jews. There was no formula in the Torah in which the Greek situation fit, and that is why Paul refers to his following advice as a concession rather than a command.

Paul goes on to explain that if a male or female (new) believer happens to be married to a spouse that does not believe, they should remain married as long as the believer's faith does not present an issue to the unbeliever and therefore creates no tension or discord in the home. Paul uses the same word in addressing both the believing man and woman as he did in verse 11 in reference to a man putting away his wife, but for the woman it is translated as "leaving" her husband (mistranslated by some as "divorce" – v.13). As previously noted, the word has a deeper meaning than simply sending someone away or leaving them; it refers to a form of neglect, or more specifically, a forsaking of something or someone. [53] Paul's instruction, then, would fall perfectly in line with what he had been taught as a Jew: a man must not unjustly send his wife away, nor should a woman unjustifiably leave her husband, as reflected in the book of Jeremiah, "Surely, as a wife *treacherously* departs from her husband, so have you dealt treacherously with Me …" (3:20, italics mine for emphasis). Again, the implication of this type of departure by the wife is one of unfaithfulness and not simply a physical departure.

If, however, the unbelieving spouse cannot stand to live with the (now) believer, then the believing spouse is under no obligation to keep the marriage (v.15). Paul finishes by stating that no believer can be guaranteed of "saving" their spouse simply by remaining in the marriage (v.16). Oddly, this reflects a common attitude among many Christian churches where abused women are encouraged to remain in their marriages because they are taught that, as long as they are submissive, their husbands will one day see the light and get saved. Unfortunately, some of these wives end up "in glory" a lot sooner than I think the good Lord wanted them to. Let us never forget, it is God's job and not ours to change people.

Paul's instruction to married believers, then, is really no different than what was upheld by the Law both in the Old Testament and by Jesus. The same principles can be summarized as follows:

1) God's ideal is for a one man/one woman lifetime relationship (according to Genesis).

2) Although this is God's ideal, this does not mean that once a man has a wife he is entitled to treat her any way he chooses. Rather, he must bond to her (cleave to his wife), nourish and protect her and treat her as he would his very own body.

3) If a husband is hard-hearted, rebellious or negligent to the point that he causes his wife personal grief, he must let her go.

4) A husband must provide for his wife according to an agreement, and if she has not committed adultery he must not malign her reputation in the eyes of others.

5) A woman therefore is not to be faulted for leaving her husband if she has been neglected or abused by him.

According to both Jewish and New Testament Bibles, then—and contrary to modern church doctrinal interpretation—divorce itself is not a sin. If *any* departure for *any* reason was considered to be sin, then Moses, Jesus and Paul would have said as much and there would be no exceptions to the rule. God wants us to live in peace. What *is* condemned in Scripture, on the part of either the husband or the wife, are sinful motives that make marriage unbearable for the other or selfishness that leads one to commit adultery or unrightfully abandon a faithful partner (see Hosea 4:14).

According to what we have read from the Scriptures, then, God wants both men and women to be in happy, fulfilling relationships. Divorce should not be the first option, especially because of the pain and conflict that arises from it. However, let us also remember that divorce is usually the end result of pain and conflict that already exists in a bad marriage situation. While divorce may have a traumatic effect on children, so does being forced to live in a household of tension, conflict and hatred. In our efforts to avoid divorce, we must also be mindful of the misery and destruction many people live through every day because of a toxic marriage. Remember, God's wants us to enjoy life, to do well, to be fulfilled and to feel safe. He is for you, not against you. I believe the key to breaking these chains is to return to the *original context* of the Bible and to put those principles into practice in our everyday life.

Part Five

APPLYING ANCIENT WISDOM TO MODERN LIFE

M odern faith movements, especially those that are Christian, claim to follow the principles of Scripture. We have seen how imbalanced many interpretations have become, especially since they have been set into the contexts of other cultures and mindsets. Does that mean that we cannot apply those same Scriptures to our own modern context? I believe we can.

The Bible is replete with principles and universal laws. When understood and applied in the light of their original intent and context, these principles are as solid as the day they were written. True principles do not change and are, by virtue of their very nature, adaptable to every time and situation.

Both Jewish and Christian Scriptures impose a higher standard on those who have, by their own free will, made a decision to invite God into their lives. That means the person of faith needs to stand out from the rest of the world. We are supposed to be salt and light. And what is the purpose in this? It is to give hope to others, since applying biblical principles to our lives should reveal the love and power of God in our lives. In other words, we should be free people and should also be striving to set others free. Unfortunately, clinging to many legalistic and archaic interpretations of Scripture causes many Christians to appear rigid, apathetic or even unsympathetic to the miseries of humanity. This is especially so concerning issues of marital conflict, the subservience of women and especially divorce. These attitudes stem from beliefs that men have the right to dominate women at will and that, regardless of the way they are treated, women are to submit in silence. Behind this interpretation is the flawed belief that God is in every marriage and that divorce is always a sin.

I personally do not believe that every marriage is ordained by God or even approved by Him. First of all, the Bible itself makes it clear in both Old and New Testaments that God's people are not to marry or intermingle with those whose beliefs directly contradict their own. The fact that this will eventually result in conflict and power struggles is evident. Being human, we are subject to misjudgments and mistakes, and we may well end up in just that situation. I even know of some women who were strongly coerced into marriages they really in their heart did not want to enter into but were either forced or overpowered to do so. This is not covenant and it is not the heart of God.

On that note, Scripture always gives a way out; in fact, its greatest and most prominent underlying message is redemption and salvation. To say otherwise is to deny the mercy and compassion of God. The church's rigid stand over the last several centuries regarding marriage and divorce has not resulted in more holiness or faith in God; instead, it has reaped resentment and unbelief toward a God who is perceived as being merciless and lacking compassion. As a result, the world's way has become more "logical" and appealing, even offering an easier way out of destructive relationships. "Shacking up" is safer than marriage— especially if you are told that you can never leave that marriage no matter how destructive it is to your life and the life of your children. And the church wonders why it is failing to reach others…

Scripture, however, does not hold only those in faith accountable. Whether or not the world accepts or realizes it, every single person on the face of this earth is subject to another principle—a responsibility to the earth and all life, especially human life. As recorded in Genesis 9:5, God declares: "Surely for your lifeblood I will demand a reckoning; from the hand of every beast I will require it, and from the hand of man. From the hand of every man's brother I will require the life of man." The Law says that the life is in the blood, so to violate someone's blood is really to harm their very life. In other words, like it or not, we will reap the effects of neglect and abuse we impose on every living thing. This also includes personal relationships. Therefore, even those who do not believe in God are obligated to fulfill the principles of love and respect as laid down by Scripture. How tragic, though, when people who claim to know God respond with less mercy and justice in their personal lives than those who do not. Is it no wonder, then, that the world does not listen when we try to tell them how wonderful God is?

I realize the teachings in this book are quite intense and perhaps difficult for some to immediately embrace. I ask that you think about what you have read and learned and seek God's face concerning the questions you may still have.

The purpose of writing this book is to bring about much needed changes. I pray it will alleviate the consciences of both men and women of faith who have had to face unjust persecution because of a failed marriage and that faith communities will be more merciful and understanding towards those who find themselves in unbearable personal and marital circumstances. I hope it will open the eyes of both partners to realize the role they each play in allowing neglect and abuse to come into their relationships. Those who are abusive or neglectful need to be held more accountable for both their actions and inactions. Women also need to once again raise their standards of expectation of the type of person with whom they choose to share their lives. A big mistake I see in this day and age is that women give themselves far too easily to men and then wonder why they do not make a commitment. If he is getting everything he wants already at no cost to him, why should he commit, especially his heart? Until women place a real sense of value on themselves, this trend of usury and self-destruction will continue. If we as individuals and as a society do not make these changes, our future generations will be doomed by our example to repeat the same mistakes, destining them to a life without fulfillment or happiness—and perhaps, even—without God.

It's time to break the chains.

ENDNOTES

1 *Beyond the Veil: Male-Female Dynamics in Modern Muslim Society,* Fatima Mernissi (1987: 53, 54).

2 *Pentateuch and Haftorahs, 2nd Edition,* Dr. J. H. Hertz, ed.; (1960: 934).

3 *Jew and Gentile in the Ancient World: Attitudes and Interactions from Alexander to Justinian,* Louis H. Feldman; (1993: 328).

4 Ibid (376, 405).

5 *Archaeology and the Old Testament,* James W. Fleming; (1999: 48).

6 Exodus 38:8.

7 *Judaism,* Arthur Hertzberg, ed.; (1961:22). This commentary is based on references throughout the Pentateuch concerning covenantal obligations, i.e. Exodus 19:5–6.

8 *The Wisdom of the Talmud: A Thousand Years of Jewish Thought,*

Rabbi Ben Zion Bokser; (1951: 18). The Talmud was compiled in the early part of the 2nd century by teachers that had settled in Jabneh after Jerusalem's fall in 70. The Great Council, or Sanhedrin, had been demolished, and so legislation was subsequently handled by local rabbis. The Talmud is a compilation of the work of these rabbis. It was meant to be a supplement to biblical Judaism, not a replacement, since the decrees were based in principle on biblical Law.

9 *Man and Woman in Christ: An Examination of the Roles of Men and Women in Light of Scripture and the Social Sciences,* Stephen B. Clark; (1980; 241).

10 Hertz; p. 932.

11 *Jesus of Nazareth: His Life, Times, and Teaching,* Joseph Klausner; (1989: 276).

12 *The Bible and the Role of Women: A Case Study in Hermeneutics,* Krister Standahl, trans. by Emilie T. Sander; (1966: 9).

13 Stephen B. Clark, (206, 207).

14 *The Apostle Paul and Women in the Church,* Don Williams; (1977: 41, 42). Although I cite this work, this was mentioned in several other sources.

15 *Man and Woman in Christ: An Examination of the Roles of Men and Women in Light of Scripture and the Social Sciences,* Stephen B. Clark; (1980: 114).

16 *A History of Christian Thought: From the Beginnings to the Council of Chalcedon, Vol. 1,* Justo L. Gonzalez; (1970: 150).

17 *The New Eve in Christ: The Use and Abuse of the Bible in the Debate About Women in the Church,* Mary Hayter; (1987: 140).

18 The belief that Mary, mother of Jesus, was born without sin and taken physically into heaven only arose hundreds of years after the time of Jesus of Nazareth. The only sources for this belief are the Apocrypha. The Apocrypha were traditionally rejected by early church and Jewish scholars for various reasons, including dispute of authorship, lack of genuineness (such as erroneous descriptions of cultural practices), and internal and external contradictions. Interestingly, these volumes were originally deemed by the Synod at Ariminum (convened by the Emperor Constatius, the son of Constantine) to be "damned from then

and now," including such books as *The Home-going of the holy Mary.* The belief that Mary ascended physically into heaven only became dogma of the Catholic Church as late as November 1, 1950, by Pope Pius XII. This is only one example of such turn-arounds in doctrine. The Catholic Church's reasons for doing this need to be addressed separately because of length of argument; however, this reference makes the point. *New Testament Apocrypha, Vol. 1,* E. Hennecke [ed. W. Schneemelcher]; (1959: 47).

19 *The Role of Women in Early Christianity: Studies in Women and Religion, Vol. 7,* Jean Laporte; (1982: 29–33), incl. references to both Tertullian and Clement.

20 Ibid (27, 28); fn 34, *De cultu feminarum,* I. CCL1, pp. 347, 350, 358; ANF 4, pp. 16, 20–21.

21 Ibid (101, 118, 119) citing the Canons of Basil and Canon 15 of the Council of Chalcedon A.D. 451.

22 Ibid (127).

23 *The Later Christian Fathers: A Selection from the writings of the Fathers from St. Cyril of Jerusalem to St. Leo the Great,* Henry Bettenson, ed. & trans.; (1970: 93). A letter from Basil to Amphilochius, Bishop of Iconium (2nd Canonical Letter, A.D. 375).

24 Ibid (7, 8, 94).

25 *The Essential Talmud,* Adin Steinsaltz; (1976: 130).

26 This is well documented in the story of Isaac and Rebekah, Genesis, chapter 24, especially v.58 (NKJV).

27 Steinsaltz, p. 130.

28 *The Hebrew-Greek Key Study Bible: Lexical Aids to the Old Testament,* Spiros Zodhiates; (1984: 1583).

29 Steinsaltz, p. 132. In fact, even female servants who ended up marrying within the master's household had the full rights of a wife (see Ex. 21:10–11).

30 Ibid.

31 *501 Hebrew Verbs,* Shmuel Bolozky (1996: 446, 447)

32 Steinsaltz, p. 131.

33 Zodhiates, p. 1592.

34 *Commentary on the Torah,* Richard Elliott Friedman; (2001: 19).

Although I cite this work, this viewpoint is quite common among Jewish sources as well as others such as Hayter in *The New Eve in Christ: The Use and Abuse of the Bible in the Debate about Women in the Church* (1987).

35 I need to make an important point here. There is so much anti-Semitism that is based on scriptures such as these that are used to "prove" that God is done with Israel. We must read the whole story, however. The separation between God and Israel was temporary, manifested by the scattering of most of the Israelites into all the parts of the world, now known as the Diaspora. Yet Jeremiah also gives the promise, as do other prophetic books, of the reconciliation between God and Israel to be evidenced by him returning them to their ancient land in the "last days." Israel was re-born in 1948, and ever since then more and more Jews are returning to their ancient roots. The "marriage," then, between God and Israel, has been reconciled.

36 This point is covered in both Bible translations by Zodhiates: *The Hebrew-Greek Key Study Bible*: 1984; pp. 1168–1169, and *The Complete Word Study New Testament: Word Study Series*: 1991; pp. 68–69.

37 Hertz, p. 933.

38 The book of Numbers (5:11–31) outlines a test of fidelity should a man suspect his wife of cheating on him. Note, however, that this was if she was not caught in the act and there were no witnesses. This instruction is also believed to have been given at a time period that superceded the original Deuteronomy instruction.

39 Hertz, p. 933.

40 Ibid, p. 932.

41 That is why Paul makes the statement in his first letter to the Corinthians: "The wife does not have authority over her own body, but the husband does. And likewise the husband does not have authority over his own body, but the wife does" (7:4). He was teaching the Greek converts the tenets of marriage based on Judaic principles. Greek men did not believe that their wives had anything to say about their sexual conduct.

42 *The Complete Word Study New Testament: Word Study Series,* Greek Dictionary of the New Testament" section, Spiros Zodhiates; (1991: 39).

43 Ibid, p. 916.

44 Ibid, p. 948.

45 *The Story of Civilization, Part III, Caesar and Christ,* Will Durant; (1944: 536, *fn* 24). Durant's footnote cites his sources, which include Schurer, Moore, Goguel and Graetz.

46 One of the main examples is when Jesus is asked whether or not it is right to pay taxes to Caesar. He responds—showing them a coin with the head of Caesar on it—to give to Caesar what is Caesar's and to God what is God's (Matthew 22:15–22).

47 The wording use in the gospels as to his reply are "except for sexual immorality or adultery," meaning that these were always considered justifiable reasons for divorce (Matthew 5:32).

48 *The Essential Talmud,* p. 133.

49 Ibid.

50 Cited in *Pentateuch and Haftorahs* (933).

51 *The Complete Word Study New Testament: Word Study Series,* Spiros Zodhiates; (1991), "Lexical Aids to the New Testament" section; p. 891 [word 630, a*poluo*].

52 Ibid, "Greek Dictionary of the New Testament" section; p. 78 (word 5563, *chorizo*).

53 Ibid, "Lexical Aids to the New Testament" section; p. 895 (word 863, *aphiemi*).

BIBLIOGRAPHY

Bokser, Rabbi Ben Zion. *The Wisdom of the Talmud: A Thousand Years of Jewish Thought.* New York: Citadel Press, 1951.

Bolozky, Shmuel. *501 Hebrew Verbs.* New York: Barron's Educational Series, Inc., 1996.

Bettenson, Henry, ed., trans. *The Later Christian Fathers.* London: Oxford University Press, 1970.

Clark, Stephen B. *Man and Woman in Christ: An Examination of the Roles of Men and Women in Light of Scripture and the Social Sciences.* Ann Arbor: Servant Books, 1980.

Daniel-Rops, Henri. *The Book of Mary,* [trans. Alastair Guinan]. New York: Hawthorn Books, Inc. 1960.

Durant, Will. *The Story of Civilization: Part III, Caesar and Christ.* New York: Simon and Schuster, 1944.

Feldman, Louis H. *Jew & Gentile in the Ancient World: Attitudes and Interactions from Alexander to Justinian.* New Jersey: Princeton University Press, 1993.

Fleming, Dr. James W. *Archaeology and the Old Testament.* Bellaire: Biblical Resources, 1999.

Fleming, Dr. James W. *Attitudes Toward Women in the Bible,* videotape series. Bellaire: Biblical Resources and First Choice Television Inc., 1999.

Friedman, Richard Elliot. *Commentary on the Torah.* New York: HarperSanFrancisco, 2001.

Gonzalez, Justo L. *A History of Christian Thought: From the Beginnings to the Council of Chalcedon, Vol. 1.* Nashville: Abingdon Press, 1970.

Hayter, Mary. *The New Eve in Christ: The Use and Abuse of the Bible in the Debate About Women in the Church.* Grand Rapids: Wm. B. Eerdmans Publishing, 1987.

Hennecke, E. [ed. W. Schneemelcher]. *New Testament Apocrypha, Vol. 1.* Philadelphia: The Westminster Press, 1959.

Hennecke, E. [ed. W. Schneemelcher]. *New Testament Apocrypha, Vol. 2.* Philadelphia: The Westminster Press, 1965.

Hertz, Dr. J. H., ed. *Pentateuch & Haftorahs, 2nd ed.* London: The Soncino Press, 1960.

Hertzberg, Arthur. *Judaism.* New York: George Braziller Publishing, 1961.

The Holy Bible (New King James Version). Nashville: Thomas Nelson Publishers, 1984.

Klausner, Joseph. *Jesus of Nazareth: His Life, Times, and Teachings,* [trans. Herbert Danby]. New York: Bloch Publishing Co., 1989.

Laporte, Jean. *The Role of Women in Early Christianity: Studies in Women and Religion, Vol. 7.* Lewiston: Mellen Press, 1982.

Matthews, Roy T., and F. DeWitt Platt. *The Western Humanities, Vol. 1: Beginnings through the Renaissance,* 4th ed. Mountain View: Mayfield Publishing Co., 2000.

Mernissi, Fatima. *Beyond the Veil: Male-Female Dynamics in Modern Muslim Society.* Bloomington, IN: Indiana University Press, 1987.

Steinsaltz, Adin. *The Essential Talmud.* [trans. Chaya Gala]. USA: Basic Books, 1976.

Stendahl, Krister. *The Bible and the Role of Women: A Case Study in Hermeneutics* [trans. Emilie T. Sander]. Philadelphia: Fortress Books, 1966.

Stern, David H. *Complete Jewish Bible.* Jerusalem: Jewish New Testament Publications, Inc., 1998.

Ward, Martha C. *A World Full of Women,* 2nd ed., Needham Heights, MA: Allyn and Bacon, 1999.

Williams, Don. *The Apostle Paul and Women in the Church.* Venture: Regal Books, 1977.

Zodhiates, Spiros, ed. *The Hebrew-Greek Key Study Bible (KJV)*. Iowa Falls: World Bible Publishers, Inc., 1984.

Zodhiates, Spiros, ed. *The Complete Word Study New Testament: Bringing the Original Text to Life*. Word Study Series. (KJV). Chattanooga, TN: AMG Publishers, 1991.